Defensive

Tips

Defensive Tips

For Bad Card Holders

Edwin B. Kantar

Griffin Publishing
Glendale, California

10 9 8 7 6 5 4 3 2 1

ISBN: 1-882180-21-6

Griffin Publishing
544 Colorado Street
Glendale, California 91204

Telephone: 1-800-423-5789

Manufactured in the United States of America

CONTENTS

CONTENTS

CONTENTS

CONTENTS

INTRODUCTION

This book was completed after the 6.8 earthquake of Jan, 1994. That is not to say that the tips are shaky, just perhaps the author.

This work completes a trilogy of tips books.The first," A Treasury of Bridge Tips"(Bidding): the second, "Take Your Tricks" (Declarer Play), and this, a collection of defensive bridge tips. I consider this to be the most important because it is in defensive play that most players are weakest.

The level ranges from intermediate to expert. Given some 580 tips, certainly some are basic; but blocking and tackling (common sense and counting) win not only football games but bridge games as well. "Advanced" tips have been noted with one asterisk(*). Advanced tips that are not standard practice have been noted with two asterisks. The ** tips come with a strong author bias and are not standard: they require PARTNERSHIP AGREEMENT.

As you might imagine it is tough to construct tips that cover every possible defensive situation. Partner's and declarer's skill level are intertwined. The right play with one partner may result in a disaster with another. Similarly you must make allowances when playing against an inexperienced declarer. Normal bidding and play inferences just don't apply.

Another problem is defensive conventions. In the past, fourth best leads, the king from ace-king and standard attitude and count were the norm. Nowadays many have shifted gears. There is a growing trend towards leading third and lowest, ace from ace-king vs. suit, as well as upside down count and attitude.

In this tome we'll assume that you lead ace from ace-king against suit contracts. This gives you a small but clear edge, provided you make all the exceptions listed. However, I am going to stick with fourth best leads as well as standard count and attitude on grounds of familiarity. However, I am convinced that upside down attitude when (1) discarding; (2) signaling with KNOWN LENGTH is superior.

If you and partner have other agreements, simply substitute your leads and signals for the ones mentioned and all will work out just fine. This book is not designed to plug one method over another (other than the ** tips). This book is designed to help you recognize and deal with common defensive situations.

As for the bidding, unless otherwise stated, common methods: Weak twos and weak jump overcalls; a strong artificial 2♣ opening with a neutral 2♦ response; limit raises; Blackwood; a 15-17 one notrump opening range plus Stayman (of course). Never mind that you have superior methods, we have to assume something. What is important is that you pay attention to THEIR bidding in order to interpret partner's leads and signals. This, in harmony with counting, is basic to good defense.

Counting is still where it's at. Counting means more than counting declarer's distribution (as early as possible), but also counting declarer's points and declarer's tricks. Counting gets easier as the play progresses and various clues are processed... providing you start at trick one!

This work supersedes everything that I have written in all other books and articles on defensive play... and then some. As you will see, some tips are followed with a complete four hand diagram. This was done to reinforce important tips with examples. Other tips are followed with a defensive problem, seeing if you can apply the tip to the problem. The remainder of the tips are either self-explanatory or are followed by a one-suit diagram as a sort of second look.

Keep in mind that even though these tips are directed at "you", you must allow for partner to be following the same tips. For example, it may be necessary for you to attack a suit with the jack holding KJx. Well, if you can do it, so can partner.

If some of these tips seem too difficult to absorb, patience. As your defense improves, these tips will begin to make more sense. After all, what good is a book if you already know everything that's in it?

I have tried not to use any great example hands from other material that I have written even though it killed me. I may have fallen from grace once or twice.

Oh yes, I did something here that I have been promising to do for years —using "she" instead of "he" in impersonal sentences.

I must finish with a special thanks to my three main editors—Ron Garber, Danny Kleinman, and Arthur Baron. NOBODY ever had a better crew.

(1)
WARM UP TIPS

1. Never, but never, forget you are playing with a partner. It pays to consider what things may look like from partner's point of view, particularly when you are privy to some information that partner isn't.

2. You cannot defend properly unless you remember the bidding.

3. You cannot defend properly unless you know what system the opponents are playing.

4. You cannot defend properly unless you watch the cards, particularly the little fellows.

5. You cannot defend properly unless you count.

6. You cannot expect your partner to defend properly if you make faces or show other signs of disapproval.

7. Keep one goal in mind: DEFEATING THE CONTRACT. Do not worry about overtricks unless you are defending a doubled contract or are playing tournament bridge.

8. A player who hesitates during the bidding is likely to have a problem hand. If that player becomes the declarer, keep the hesitation in mind.

9. The figure to focus on during the defense is the number of tricks you need at any given moment to defeat the contract. Defense is based on this figure.

10. Give your opening lead a little consideration. The fate of many a contract is determined by that one card. Use the bidding as a guide.

11. Make sure you and your partner are on the same wave length concerning leads and signaling conventions.

12. Don't compound a crime. If you, or more likely partner, have made an error, do not lose your cool. Many contracts can still be beaten after one defensive error, seldom after TWO.

13. If partner makes a nice play, a kind word or two at the end of the hand goes a long way.

14. The speed of the play may be a clue to declarer's problem. When playing a 4-3 trump fit, play usually slows to a crawl.

15. When two possible defenses present themselves to defeat the contract, both equally likely, select the simpler. (Unless you are looking to make an appearance in a newspaper column.)

16. If you can see the winning defense, take charge. Don't put any additional pressure on partner if you don't have to.

17. Keep partner's skill level in mind. Lead a poor player by the hand.

18. Watch partner's spot card signals. The stronger your partner, the more meaningful they are.

20. Keep your singletons and doubletons in the middle of your hand. Some players watch where your cards come from.

21. Try not to guard against non-existent dangers; guard only against those that are consistent with the bidding and play.

22. Try to put yourself in declarer's shoes. If you can discern her fears, play on those fears though they may not be realistic.

(2)

THE OPENING LEAD (VS. SUIT)

The card you select as your opening lead is probably the most important card you are going to play during the entire defense. Therefore, you should give it a little thought. Your focus should be on the likely distribution around the table (easier when there is plenty of bidding), declarer's likely strength and the degree of trump fit that the bidding seems to indicate. Of major concern is whether you should be making an aggressive or a passive opening lead. Again you must go back to the bidding to help you out. Does the dummy figure to have a long side suit? If there is a long side suit, how is it breaking? Should I be looking to ruff? Should I be looking to give partner a ruff? Should I be trying to shorten the declarer? Should I just be sitting back and waiting for tricks rather than attacking here, there, and everywhere? Should I be leading a trump to cut down ruffs in the dummy? These are some of the questions you should be asking yourself before you make your opening lead.

TRUMP LEADS

23. Don't even think of leading a trump when the opponents are in the throes of a misfit.

24. Holding a balanced hand with broken strength in each suit, a trump lead from two or three small when dummy has given a single raise is usually best.

25. Avoid leading a singleton trump unless partner has passed a one level takeout double announcing a strong trump holding. If she has, a trump lead is mandatory.

26. If partner is marked with a singleton trump, there is no point in leading a trump from Kxx because neither of you will be able to continue the suit. Try another lead and hope that partner will find the trump switch, if necessary.

27* To give count in trump lead low from an even number, high-low with an odd number (lead the three from 732 or 86532).

28** When dummy has shown a long side suit plus trump support, lead a trump if you have the side suit well bottled up-even if partner has bid.

29. Leading low from Axx or Kxx is a reasonably safe lead; leading a low trump from Jxx or Qxx is far more dangerous. Lead low from J10x in case partner has a singleton honor. If a trump lead is called for, lead a trump from almost any holding.

30. Deceptive leads in the trump suit include the nine from 109x and the jack from QJ doubleton.

31. When your side has the majority of the high card strength a trump lead to cut down dummy's ruffing power is usually best.

32. When declarer has bid two suits and you are strong in one, but dummy prefers the other, lead a trump to cut down dummy's ruffing power.

33. Trump leads are frequently effective when dummy is known to be 4-4-4-1 and the opponents appear to be playing a 4-4 trump fit.

SHORT SUIT LEADS

34. Short suit leads tend to work out best when holding a certain trump entry. (Ax, Axx or Kxx). Short suit leads seldom work out if ruffing will cost you a natural trump trick. (QJx, QJ9x, J10xx, etc)

35. Holding an ace do not lead a singleton in an unbid suit vs. a VOLUNTARILY bid SMALL slam . Partner won't have an ace. It is far wiser to lead a singleton when you do not hold an ace. Partner may have the ace of your singleton suit or the ace of trump.

36. Do not lead a singleton in an unbid suit vs. a voluntarily bid GRAND slam. The worst.

37. When both you and partner have each shown strong suits and partner leads one of their suits, think singleton with a likely trump entry.

LEADING PARTNER'S SUIT

38. With a weak hand and Qxxx(x) or Kxxx(x) lead the honor in case you need to switch to another suit. If you lead low, you may never get in again.

39. With the ace and any length, lead the ace unless you feel you must get partner in at once to: (1) give you a ruff; (2) lead a suit through declarer before another suit can be established. Underleads of aces when they don't work out require a very special relationship with partner.

40. With 10xx, Jxx, or Qxx lead low. However if dummy has bid notrump, lead the high honor.

41. With three or four small, lead low if you have NOT supported; high if you have.

42. If you have led high from xxx, play your middle card next. If you have led high from xxxx, play your lowest card next. If you have led low from xxx, play your highest card next. If you have led low from xxxx, play your lowest card next.

43. Leading a suit partner has overcalled is USUALLY safer than leading a suit partner has opened. However, if the bidding has indicated that partner has made a light third hand opening, tend to lead partner's suit. One reason for opening light in third seat is to attract the lead.

LEADS VS. DOUBLED CONTRACTS

44. When partner doubles the final contract, partner either:

(1) Thinks that the combined defensive strength between the two defensive hands is enough to defeat the contract.

(2) Has a strong trump holding.

(3) Can tell from the bidding that it is a touch and go contract and that you have trump length. The double is an effort to give declarer a false impression of who has the missing trump. These are called "offside" doubles and also require a special relationship with partner when they don't work.

(4) Is trying to direct your lead to a particular suit, a suit you might not otherwise have led. These "lead directing" doubles apply vs. slam contracts or when partner has preempted.

45. When partner makes a penalty double, assume partner is short in your long suit. Penalty doubles work best when the doubling side is misfitted.

LEADS VS. DOUBLED SLAM CONTRACTS

46. If partner has bid and later doubles a VOLUNTARILY bid slam, do NOT lead partner's suit (the normal lead) and do NOT lead a trump. Partner's double shows either:

(1) A void (the most common reason).

(2) A desire for a lead in dummy's first bid suit.

(3) The AK of one of declarer's bid suits.

If partner has NOT bid and later doubles a VOLUNTARILY bid slam, do not lead the unbid suit. (That is the normal lead).

Partner's double shows either:

(1) a side suit void

(2) a desire for the lead in dummy's first bid suit.

LEADING VS. A SLAM WHEN THERE IS NO DOUBLE TO HELP YOU OUT

47. If dummy makes a wild leap to slam (no Blackwood), assume a void, strong trump, a long powerful side suit and a likely control in the shorter side suit. It is usually right to lead that shorter side suit.

North	**East**	**South**	**West** (you)
1♥	Pass	1♠	2♣
6♠!	All Pass		

You hold: ♠ A43 ♥ Q5 ♦ J64 ♣ AQJ95

Dummy certainly has a club void with a long heart suit. Lead a diamond and hope to build up a trick in that suit before your ♠A is removed.

48. If the opponents go through Blackwood, and partner has a chance to double an artificial response(s) and doesn't, assume partner has no great strength in that suit(s).

South	**West**(you)	**North**	**East**
1♠	Pass	3♠	Pass
4NT	Pass	5♦	Pass
5NT	Pass	6♣	Pass
6♠	All Pass		

Partner had a chance to double 5♦ and 6♣ and did not. Keep that in mind before making your opening lead.

HONOR CARD LEADS

49. If you normally lead the Ace from AKx(x), lead the KING if:

(1) Partner has bid or raised the suit.

(2) The opponents are playing at the five or six level.

(3) FROM TRICK TWO ON.

(4) You have AK doubleton.

** (5) You have bid the suit and are planning to shift to a singleton at Trick 2.

50. If you normally lead the king from AKx(x), lead the ACE if:

(1) You hold AK doubleton.

(2) You have an unsupported seven or eight card suit. If partner is void, she may ruff your king.

51** A convention worth considering is the lead of the Q from AKQ in any suit that has been bid strongly or from a player with a known strong hand.

52. Avoid leading aces in unsupported suits unless:

(1) You are short (5' 2" or less). This is actually a serious book, you'll see. (A or Ax)

(2) You have bid the suit and partner has not supported.

(3) The opponents have bid everything under the sun except notrump and ended in a minor suit contract.

INFERENCES

53. If partner doesn't lead your suit, assume partner:

(1) Is void.

(2) Has a side suit singleton.

(3) Has a side suit sequence.

(4) Has the ace and fears declarer may have the king.

(5) Has forgotten the bidding.

54. If partner has a chance to double an artificial bid, (Stayman, Jacoby, cuebids), particularly at a high level, and doesn't, you should probably look elsewhere for the killing lead.

55. If you can infer shortness in partner's hand and you have a quick trump entry, lead partner's short suit (with a suit preference card, if possible).

North	**East**	**South**	**West** (you)
1♦	Pass	1♠	Pass
2♣	Pass	3♦	Pass
3♠	Pass	4♠	All Pass

You hold: ♠ A ♥ A932 ♦ 9543 ♣ Q1043

Lead the ♦9 to show a heart entry. In fact, you should double and lead a diamond.

56. If partner prefers the second of two suits you have bid, assume shortness in the first. (Good thinking). However, if partner leads your second suit, play partner for a trump holding that is not looking for a ruff. (See tip 32)

57* When making a blind lead, don't be looking for miracles in any suit partner could have overcalled at the ONE level and didn't.

58. When you have a poor hand, partner hasn't bid and the opponents stop at the one or two level, assume partner has strength in the opponents' first bid suit(s)—or the opponents don't know how to bid.

59. When the opponents voluntarily bid game and you have an opening bid or better, no need to look across the table to see how despondent partner is. Consider yourself lucky if partner has as much as a queen.

60. If it is CLEAR dummy has a void, underleading an ace in that suit usually works. However, if dummy turns up with a singleton and declarer has the king, don't call and don't write.

61. When partner does not lead the unbid suit and is not leading a singleton or from a sequence, chances are partner has the ace of the unbid suit.

62. If partner makes a daring underlead and you find yourself unexpectedly on play, chances are partner has a side suit void.

MISCELLANEOUS

63. Holding four trump (or suspecting partner does) and defending against a likely 5-3 or 5-2 trump fit, go for the forcing game and lead from length in the hope of shortening declarer. If forced to ruff twice, declarer is apt to lose control of the hand.

South	**West**(you)	**North**	**East**
1♠	Pass	2♣	Pass
2♠	Pass	4♠	All Pass

You hold: (1) ♠ A843 ♥ K10543 ♦ 84 ♣ 75
(2) ♠ A83 ♥ K10543 ♦ 84 ♣ 753

With (1) lead a low heart. You have four trump and your objective is a forcing defense

With (2) lead a top diamond. With ♠ Axx your goal is a diamond ruff.

64. When the opponents have a fit and there are two unbid side suits, lead from the stronger. However, if one unbid is headed by an ace, lead from the other. If both unbids have equal strength (KJxx vs. KJxxx) lead from the shorter.

South	West (you)	North	East
1♠	Pass	2♦	Pass
2♠	Pass	3♠	Pass
4♠	All Pass	Pass	Pass

You hold: (1) ♠ 54 ♥ AJ54 ♦ 876 ♣ J1076
(2) ♠ 54 ♥ K1054 ♦ 876 ♣ K832

With (1) lead the ♣J (the suit that does not have the ace).
With (2) lead a low heart (the stronger unbid).

65. After having shown a long suit during the bidding, an unnatural lead in that suit indicates a side suit void.

West (you)	North	East	South
3♠	Dbl.	4♠	6♥
All Pass			

Your hand: ♠ KJ97632 ♥ 65 ♦ J1087 ♣ -
Lead the ♠2, an impossible card, to indicate a club void; with a diamond void, lead the ♠ 9.

66. Avoid leading low from length without an honor.

Lead high from three or four small when:

(1) You have made a takeout double.

(2) Declarer has shown a two-suiter with at least 10 cards in two suits and you are leading one of declarer's short suits.

(3) You are leading a suit you have supported.

67. When the opponents have explored 3NT and wound up in five of a minor, tend to lead the unbid suit. Chances are neither opponent has a stopper in that suit.

South	West(you)	North	East
1♦	Pass	3♦	Pass
3♥	Pass	3♠	Pass
5♦	All Pass		

Your hand: ♠ J86 ♥ 10543 ♦ 64 ♣ AQ76

Lead the ♣A; partner is almost sure to have the ♣K. If either opponent had the king, notrump would have been bid eons ago.

68* If you and partner have any lead directing bids, trot them out when possible.

South	**West** (you)	**North**	**East**
Pass	Pass	1♠	2♥
3♠	?		

Your hand: ♠ 4 ♥ J765 ♦ AK103 ♣ 8743

If you play that a new suit at the FOUR level by a PASSED HAND is lead directing with support for partner's suit, bid 4♦.

69. Don't look a gift horse in the mouth. If they deal you a newspaper column opening lead (a suit headed by the AKQ, AKJ, KQJ or QJ10), be prepared for a chilly postmortem if you lead something else.

70. If dummy has a known five or six card side suit, double check your holding in that suit. With the "death" holdings, (Qxx, Kxx, KJx), make an attacking lead. However, with a strong holding such as KQ10x(x), there is less of an urgency to make an attacking lead. A trump lead to cut down down ruffs may be better.

71. No matter how badly your lead or partner's lead has turned out, no faces!

(3)
THE OPENING LEAD (VS. NOTRUMP)

You should have a good reason for NOT leading from your longest suit, but there are plenty: (1) the opponents may have bid the suit; (2) a known long suit is coming down in dummy and a stronger attacking lead from KQx or AKx may be called for; (3) you can infer that dummy has length in the suit. Additionally, when you finally decide which suit to lead, you want to make it clear to partner what you have in that suit. It is presumed that you have discussed the meaning of your honor card leads as well as the lead of the nine.

72. Fourth best from your longest and strongest will get you through many lead problems, but not enough to make it a blind rule.

73. The lead of a low card shows strength. Do NOT lead low from three or four small in an unbid suit; lead high. When your top card is an eight or lower, lead the eight.When your top card is a nine, lead second best from four but the nine from 98xx or 9xx. Holding 10xxx, lead second best if you want another suit returned; otherwise lead fourth best. Lead the ten from 10xx if you want another suit returned otherwise lead low.

74. If your fourth highest card in an UNBID suit is a seven or an eight (AQ98x, KJ97x) you might consider leading low to avoid confusion, particularly with an inexperienced partner. (See previous tip)

HONOR CARD LEADS (THE TEN)

75** Playing "standard", the lead of the ten shows either top of a sequence or suits headed by the A109, K109 or Q109. The tip is to lead fourth best from four or five card suits headed by the A109, K109, or Q109 if the FOURTH highest card is a six or lower. Lead the 10 from K1098(x) or Q1097(x) but lead the six from A1096x.

If you play "jack denies, nine or ten implies" the lead of the ten is either top of a sequence or from combinations headed by the AJ10 or KJ10. With A109, K109 or Q109 combinations, lead the nine unless the fourth highest card is a six or lower. If it is, lead fourth best.

HONOR CARD LEADS (THE JACK)

76. If you play "standard", the lead of the jack shows either top of a sequence, shortness or suits headed by the AJ10 or KJ10.

If you play "jack denies", the lead of the jack is top of a sequence or shortness, period. Lead the ten from AJ10 or KJ10 combinations.

Which method is better? Some experts do not like "jack denies" because they feel it gives declarer too much information. (It also gives partner more information). These very same experts prefer leading third and lowest vs. suit because it gives partner more information. Go figure. "Jack denies" is definitely easier on the nervous system.

HONOR CARD LEADS (THE QUEEN)

77. Lead the queen from QJ10(x)(x) or QJ9(x)(x). If the card under the jack is an eight or lower, (QJ8x(x), lead fourth best. The queen is also led from AQJx(x). Some also lead the queen from KQ109(x) asking for an unblock of the jack.

HONOR CARD LEADS (THE KING)

78. Lead the king from sequences headed by the KQJ or KQ10. Other possibilities include AKx(x) or KQx. A good case can also be made for leading the king from combinations headed by the KQ98 or KQ9xx(x) with an outside entry.

HONOR CARD LEADS (THE ACE)

79. This is the strongest lead and is generally made when the opening leader has 100 honors in the suit: AKQ10(x), AKJ10(x) or AQJ10(x). The lead asks for an unblock. However, if dummy or declarer has shown a long, strong suit, the lead of the ace does NOT ask for an unblock. it might simply be a desperation attempt to "find" partner. Note: Some play that the king is the stronger lead and reserve the lead of the ace for AKx(x).

80. Holding two non-touching honors with three card length and hoping to "hit" partner's length and strength, lead the lower honor. The queen from AQx, the jack from AJx and KJx, and the ten from A10x, K10x or Q10x.

81. Lead the ace from AQ109x(x) or AK109(x)(x) with an outside entry; with no outside entry, lead the nine or ten depending upon agreement.

LEADING A SUIT BID BY THE OPPONENTS

82* When leading from length in a suit bid by the opponents, lead FOURTH BEST from holdings such as KQJxx, KQ10xx, QJ10xx, QJ9xx, J109xx or J108xx. Leading low from one of these sequences presumes an outside entry. The idea is not to block the suit or crash honors in case partner has a singleton or doubleton honor.

I tried this tip out recently and this is what happened:

Both sides vul.
Dealer South

North (dummy)
♠ 8
♥ AQJ2
♦ 932
♣ QJ876

West (author)
♠ J10932
♥ 64
♦ AJ5
♣ 732

East
♠ AQ4
♥ 10987
♦ K1076
♣ 95

South
♠ K763
♥ K53
♦ Q84
♣ AK10

South	West	North	East
1NT	Pass	2♣	Pass
2♠	Pass	3NT	All Pass

Opening lead: ♠3

When I saw the ♠8, my heart stopped. Don't tell me declarer has the AKQx and that miserable singleton ♠8 is going to win a trick. Worse. Partner, naturally enough,thought my spades were stronger and played the ♠Q. Declarer won and claimed ten tricks. Strangely enough it takes a spade lead (followed by a diamond shift) at trick two to defeat the hand. Was it my fault for leading the wrong spade? If I had led the jack, would partner be smart enough to win and return a diamond? Actually, it wasn't anybody's fault. Some hands are just not meant to be beaten.The sooner you can live with that the better.

83. When leading a suit in which declarer's length is known, it is not necessary to lead fourth best. It is usually better to lead your lowest card for two reasons:

(1) Fourth best may be wasteful.

(2) Why tell declarer your length when partner already knows it?

LEAD DIRECTING DOUBLES

84. Negative inferences abound when the opponents use Stayman, Jacoby, or bid the fourth suit (usually an artificial bid), and partner does NOT double. Look elsewhere when in doubt.

South	**West** (you)	**North**	**East**
1NT	Pass	2♣	Pass
2♥	Pass	3NT	All Pass

You hold: ♠ J6432 ♥ A43 ♦ 864 ♣ 93

Dummy is known to have four spades so that's out. Leading a heart into declarer doesn't look too clever either. Partner had a chance to double 2♣ and didn't. The winner, by elimination: a top diamond.

85. Most partnerships have rules governing lead-directing doubles of final notrump contracts. If ever there was an area for discussion, this is it. What follows are several non-controversial tips, followed by several controversial ones. The controversial ones are marked with an **. (Don't try a ** double on partner without prior discussion!).

86. If partner doubles a final notrump contract and NO suits have been bid, partner indicates a solid suit (usually a major). It's your job to decide which suit it is. Begin by eliminating any suit in which you have the jack or better.

87. If neither you nor your partner has bid, partner's double calls for dummy's first bid suit.

88** If partner opens 1♥ or 1♠, has no chance to bid again at the two level and eventually doubles a final notrump contract, lead a lower ranking suit.

East	**South**	**West** (you)	**North**
1♥	1NT	Pass	3NT
Dbl.	All Pass		

You hold: ♠ Q1043 ♥ 82 ♦ 76 ♣ J9432

Lead a high diamond, partner's likely second suit.

89** If partner overcalls at the ONE level, has no chance to bid again at the two level, and eventually doubles a final three notrump contract, do not lead partner's suit. Either lead dummy's first bid suit or a lower ranking suit. Your hand should tell you which.

North	**East**	**South**	**West** (you)
1♥	1♠	2NT	Pass
3NT	Dbl.	All Pass	

You hold (a) ♠ 95 ♥ Q10765 ♦ J543 ♣ 106
(b) ♠ 5 ♥ 104 ♦ QJ432 ♣ J8754

With (a) lead the ♣10 as partner cannot be asking for a heart; with (b) lead the ♥10 as partner cannot be asking for a lower ranking suit.

90. If partner overcalls at the two or three level and you haven't bid, lead partner's suit.

91** When both you, partner and dummy have all bid different suits, lead dummy's suit if it was bid at the ONE level; your suit if dummy's first bid suit was at the two level. If partner wants a lead in her own suit, partner should pass as that is the expected lead.

92. Doubles of notrump slams generally call for dummy's first bid suit.

INFERENCES

93. When the responder to a one or two notrump opening bid does NOT use Stayman, the inference is no four card major. Be leery of leading a broken five card minor when Stayman is NOT used. Too often you will be running into dummy's length.

South	**West (you)**	**North**	**East**
1NT	Pass	3NT	All Pass

You hold: ♠ Q962 ♥ A32 ♦ J8643 ♣ 2

Try the ♠2 rather than the ♦4.

94. When the responder uses Stayman and then bids 3NT after partner has shown a major, responder is presumed to have the other major. Do not lead dummy's major with a broken four or five card holding in that major. It makes more sense to lead through dummy's four card major with a doubleton. Partner is marked with at least four cards in the suit.

South	**West**(you)	**North**	**East**
1NT	Pass	2♣	Pass
2♠	Pass	3NT	All Pass

You hold: (a) ♠ A632 ♥ Q653 ♦ J982 ♣ 5
(b) ♠ A632 ♥ J10 ♦ 10653 ♣ Q76

With (a) lead the ♦2; with (b) the ♥J.

95. When trying to find partner's suit, tend to exclude any suit partner might have overcalled at the ONE level and did not.

North	**East**	**South**	**West** (you)
1♥	Pass	2NT	Pass
3NT	All Pass		

You hold: ♠ 94 ♥ KJ5432 ♦ 1094 ♣ J10

Better to lead a minor than a spade. Partner had a chance to overcall 1♠ and didn't.

MISCELLANEOUS

96. Consider partner's likely high card strength before making your lead. The bidding may warn you that partner has zilch!

North	**East**	**South**	**West** (you)
Pass	Pass	1NT	Pass
3NT	All Pass		

You hold: ♠ J432 ♥ 1094 ♦ AQJ ♣ AK10

The opponents figure to have all the missing 25 HCP, leaving poor partner with none. Lead the ♥10 and play the waiting game.

97. With three or four small in partner's suit, lead low if you have not supported, high if you have; with honor third, lead low.

98. With two equally desirable suits, lead from the one that does NOT have the ace. You may be able to use the ace as the entry to the other suit once it is finally set up. (In any case that is what you plan to tell partner when it turns out you have led the wrong suit.)

South	**West** (you)	**North**	**East**
1NT	2♣*	3NT	All Pass

* Majors

Your hand: ♠ K10843 ♥ A9743 ♦ J2 ♣ 4
Lead the ♠4.

99. With a choice of two suits to lead, lead from the stronger. (Prefer Q10xx to Kxxx.)

100. When you are particularly strong in a suit (AQJx) but do not want to lead the suit for fear of giving declarer a cheap trick, lead a discouraging card in another suit.

South	**West** (you)	**North**	**East**
1NT	Pass	3NT	All Pass

♠ AQJ9 ♥ 10763 ♥ 92 ♣ J76

Lead the ♥7. If you lead the ♥3, partner may return hearts for all eternity — and then some.

101. If you conventionally lead the Q from KQ109(x) asking for an unblock of the jack, make an exception if dummy or declarer has known length. Partner, holding the ace, may misread the lead, overtake, and return another suit.

102. One way to help partner out on lead is to make relatively light ONE level overcalls with good suits. Some partners need more help than others.

103* Tricky or deceptive leads are most often made with strong hands. Partner, with a likely yarborough, won't be involved, and declarer may be fooled. Holding : ♠ A8732 ♥ A65 ♦ Q4 ♣ QJ6 try the ♠2 instead of the ♠3 if the bidding has gone 1NT-3NT or 2NT-3NT.

104. Lead the same vs. 4NT as you would vs. 3NT. Leading vs. 6NT is a horse of a different color.

South	**West** (you)	**North**	**East**
1NT	Pass	3NT,4NT,6NT	

You hold: ♠ J54 ♥ A1084 ♦ 1094 ♣ 954
Vs. 3NT or 4NT lead the ♥4, but vs. 6NT, try the ♦10. It is seldom right to underlead (or lead) an ace vs. 6NT.

105. Be reluctant to lead from a four card suit headed by the AQxx. However, low from AQxxx is a very strong lead.

106. The lead of a strong three card sequence is usually preferable to fourth best from a weak four card suit. (QJ10 is preferable to Jxxx).

107. If you are planning to lead dummy's first bid suit and have a gut feeling that declarer has a singleton, it may pay to lead high from strongish holdings headed by the K or A in case declarer has a singleton honor.

	North (dummy)	
	Q754	
West (you)		**East**
K1083		A962
	South	
	J	

Here the lead of the king strikes gold. (Of course it does, I constructed it that way). If declarer has the singleton ace, cheer up, there are other tips in this book that actually work.

(4)
THIRD HAND VS. SUIT

Just as the opening lead is partner's "big moment", so it is with your play to the first trick. A significant number of contracts are decided by third hand play at trick one. Even though you may think you have an obvious play, it pays to take your time and review what you think you know about declarer's hand, etc. Taking a few seconds also gives partner a chance to get organized and do a little counting. In order to make the right play at trick one, you must have some idea whether partner is leading from length or shortness, weakness or strength. Do not be a slave to "third hand high" and "always return partner's suit."

Try to make your signals clear, not wishy-washy. Partner, on the other hand, must keep in mind that it is easier for you to give a clearer signal from length (K107643) than from shortness (1098).

Other things to consider are: (1) the expected lead from the bidding compared to the actual lead; (2) partner's likely trump length; (3) whether an unusually strong or unusually weak dummy tables. Versus a strong dummy, think aggressively and imaginatively; vs. a weak dummy, think more conservatively.

THIRD HAND HIGH

108. When partner leads low, presumably from length, and there are NO honor cards in dummy, play your highest card; with equal high cards, play your lower or lowest equal.

North (dummy)
975

West
2

East (you)
AJ4 (A)
KQ84 (Q)
QJ104 (10)
J1086 (6)

South
?

In the last example, if the five is played from dummy, the six is equal to the jack.

THIRD HAND NOT SO HIGH

109. When partner leads low, presumably from length, and dummy has Jxx(x) or Qxx(x) and plays low, if you hold the queen or king, play your next highest card if it is the NINE OR TEN. If it isn't, play third hand high.

(a)

North (dummy)
Q72 or J72

West
3

East (you)
K106 (10)
K96 (9)
K86 (K)
K986 (6)

South
?

In the last example, the six is equal to the nine.

110. When you have the ace and dummy the jack, play the ACE. When you have the ace and dummy has the queen or king and plays low, insert your next highest card if it is the TEN OR JACK. If it isn't, play third hand high.

(a)

North (dummy)
J75

West
2

East (you)
A104 (A)
A943 (A)

(b)

North (dummy)
K75, Q75

West
2

East (you)
AJ63 (J)
A106 (10)
A96 (A)*

* There are times when dummy has the king (and occasionally the queen), when the play of the nine is the stronger play. There are no simple tips to spell this one out, you are on your own. Sorry.

111. When partner leads low and dummy has the highest visible honor, and plays low, play as if dummy had small cards.

	North (dummy)	
	A75	
West		**East** (you)
2		K108 (K)
		KQ8 (Q)
		J10 (10)
		J1096 (9)

THIRD HAND LOWER STILL

112. Many third hand plays are based on the assumption that partner is NOT underleading an ace at trick one. If you can't see the ace, assume declarer has it and play accordingly.

(a)

	North (dummy)	
	KJ5	
West		**East** (you)
10742		Q93 (9)
	South	
	A86	

If partner leads low and dummy plays low, insert the nine.

(b)

	North (dummy)	
	K104	
West		**East** (you)
Q932		J85 (8)
	South	
	A76	

If partner leads low and dummy plays low, insert the eight and hope it drives out the ace.

THIRD HAND ROCK BOTTOM

113. If partner leads from weakness and you have no promotable cards in the suit, play low.

(a)

	North (dummy)	
	KJ109	
West		**East** (you)
83		Q7642 (2)
	South	
	A5	

Once an East who was South's sole heir covered dummy's nine thinking to increase her inheritance. South, seeing how East squandered her honor cards, felt she would do the same with material wealth, and promptly disinherited her.

(b)

	North (dummy	
	K64	
West		**East** (you)
93		J752 (2)
	South	
	AQ108	

Not only is it foolish to play the jack when partner leads the nine, it is misleading. After the jack loses, partner will assume you have a higher honor; play low.

(c)

	North (dummy)	
	AK95	
West		**East** (you)
103		J764
	South	
	Q82	

The principle of not playing third hand high when it can be of no help, extends beyond trick one. Assume partner leads the ten which is taken in dummy. Later when partner leads the three and dummy plays low, play low and block the suit.

THIRD HAND QUANDARIES

114. When partner's lead is ambiguous, go back to the bidding to try to sort it out. If that doesn't help, play for the holding that gives you the better chance of defeating the contract.

(a)

	North (dummy)	
	A983	
West		**East** (you)
2		Q1075
	South	
	?	

Partner leads the deuce and dummy plays low. What to do? If partner has Kxx (and declarer Jx), the queen is the winning play. If partner has led a singleton and declarer has KJ64, the seven is the stronger play.

(b)

	North (dummy)	
	Q4	
West		**East** (you)
2		A106
	South	
	?	

Another toughie. Partner leads low and dummy plays low. If partner has led from the king, the ace is the winning play; if partner has led from the jack, the ten is the stronger play.

Both sides vul.
Dealer South

North (dummy)
♠ 2
♥ Q976
♦ Q4
♣ AK10974

East (you)
♠ 9765
♥ 108
♦ A106
♣ 8532

South	**West**	**North**	**East**
2♣	Pass	3♣	Pass
3♠	Pass	4♣	Pass
4♠	Pass	5♠	Pass
6♠	All Pass		

Opening lead: ♦2 (fourth best) Dummy plays low, which diamond do you play?

The 10. You should reason that South must have the ♦K to justify the 6♠ bid and could easily have a club void. If you played the ♦10 at trick and returned a trump upon winning the ♦A, +200. If you played the ♦A at trick one, -1430.

South's hand: ♠ AKQJ1084 ♥ AK ♦ K953 ♣ -
Partner's hand: ♠ 3 ♥ J5432 ♦ J872 ♣ QJ6

Both sides vul.
Dealer South

North (dummy)
♠ A2
♥ KQ75
♦ 10876
♣ K43

East (you)
♠ 965
♥ A832
♦ -
♣ QJ10972

South	West	North	East
2♠	3♦	3♠	All Pass

Opening lead: ♥9 (Dummy plays low), plan your defense.

Win and return a high heart (suit preference for diamonds). Even though it is unlikely that declarer would open 2♠ holding four hearts, how else do you propose to get five tricks?

Opener's hand: ♠ QJ10843 ♥ J1064 ♦ KQ ♣ 5
Partner's hand: ♠ K7 ♥ 9 ♦ AJ95432 ♣ A86

115. When partner's spot card lead is ambiguous, take a good look at all of the spot cards you can see. By the process of elimination, you may be able to sort it out after all.

North (dummy)
J64

West
3

East (you)
AK72

South
5

Playing fourth best leads, you win the opening lead with the king. Who has the queen? Partner is a big favorite to hold the queen. **South** cannot hold Q5 because partner would have led the ten, not the three, from 10983. Nor can declarer have Q85 because partner would have led the 10 from 1093. Only if partner has led the three from 1083 can declarer hold the queen.

116. When partner's lead of a low card can either be low from three small or a singleton, and you have the luxury of cashing an outside ace first to get a verifying signal, by all means do so.

East-West vul.
Dealer East

North (dummy)
♠ 109
♥ 9842
♦ J85
♣ KJ106

East (you)
♠ J76
♥ 65
♦ AQ9
♣ AQ984

East	**South**	**West**	**North**
1♣	1♥	Dbl.	2♥
Pass	4♥	All Pass	

Opening lead: ♣2 Dummy plays the ten and you win the queen. What now?

As it is not clear whether partner has led from a singleton or three small clubs, you should cash the ♦A to find out. If partner signals encouragement, continue with a low diamond. If partner signals discouragement, play the ace and a club.

Declarer's hand: ♠ AK42 ♥ AKQ107 ♦ 6 ♣ 753
Partner's hand: ♠ Q853 ♥ J3 ♦ K107432 ♣ 2

With the actual layout, partner will play the ♦2 to make life very easy for you.

DISCOVERY PLAYS

117* A nifty way to decode partner's spot card opening lead is to make a "discovery" play. There are two common positions:

North (dummy)
876

West
x

East (you)
AQ5

South
?

When partner leads low and there is no chance you can lose your ace, and it is important to find out quickly who has the king play the queen. A discovery play is also available when partner leads low, dummy has small cards and you have KJx(x). If it is important that YOU know immediately who has the queen, play the jack.

East-West vul.
Dealer North

North (dummy)
♠ 42
♥ 853
♦ K52
♣ KQJ102

East (you)
♠ QJ65
♥ KJ6
♦ 43
♣ A875

North	**East**	**South**	**West**
Pass	Pass	1♦	Pass
2♣	Pass	3♦	Pass
4♦	Pass	5♦	All Pass

Opening lead: ♥2   Plan your defense

Play the ♥J at trick one to smoke out the queen. When in with the ♣A you are going to have to decide whether to continue hearts or shift to the ♠Q. The card declarer plays to the first trick will solve your problem. If declarer wins with the queen, shift to a spade; if declarer wins with the ace, continue hearts.

MAKING ASSUMPTIONS FROM WHAT IS NOT LED

118. When you can't see the ace or the king of an unbid suit, assume the honors are split or declarer has them both.

To a slightly lesser degree make the same assumption when you can't see the king or queen of an unbid suit.

119. When partner bids a suit and doesn't lead it and you can't see AKQ of the suit, assume partner has the AQ and declarer the king.

120. Assume partner is not underleading a KQ combination (or the ace) at trick one. This translates into NOT playing the jack when dummy tables with A10x(x).

North (dummy)
A103

West
K872

East (you)
J64

South
Q95

When partner leads low and dummy plays low, show big time class and play the four! Even though South wins the trick with the five, your play saves a trick. The suit is now "frozen". (See tip 539).

THIRD HAND PLAY WITH EQUALS

121. After having played the lowest equal from three or four equals, play your highest equal next.

North (dummy)
763

West
84

East (you)
KQJ102 (10) (K)

South
A95

If partner leads the eight, play the ten. Your second play in the suit should be the king.

122. When signaling encouragement with equal spot cards, signal with the higher or the highest equal.

North (dummy)
Q63

West
1092

East (you)
K875 (8)

South
AJ4

Partner leads the ten and dummy plays low. Signal with the EIGHT, not the seven. The seven DENIES the eight. In this position if you signal with the seven, partner will be afraid to continue the suit fearing declarer has AJ8(x).

123* When taking a trick with equals, use the lower or the lowest equal.

North (dummy)
1065

West
KQ4

East (you)
AJ83

South
972

Partner leads the king, queen and then low. Win the third round with the JACK. Winning with the ace denies the jack and gives partner a false impression. However, if partner is oblivious, or declarer is sure to ruff, play the ace.

124. When TAKING a trick with an equal honor DOUBLETON, win with the higher equal if you are planning on returning the suit.

(a)

North (dummy)
1065

West
J9732

East (you)
AK

South
Q84

To show a doubleton, play the ace and then the king.

(b)

North (dummy)
A65

West
J974

East (you)
KQ

South
10832

Partner leads low and dummy plays low; win the king and return the queen to show a doubleton.

125* With equal honors doubleton if dummy plays low, play your lower equal when you have no assurance of winning the trick; but if dummy takes the trick, play the higher equal.

North (dummy)
K85

West
107432

East (you)
QJ

South
A96

If dummy plays low, play the jack as declarer is marked with the ace and you have no assurance of winning the trick. If dummy plays the king, play the queen.

WHEN PARTNER LEADS AN HONOR

126* When partner leads an honor (other than from AKx(x)), and you have a small doubleton, play LOW unless:

(1) Partner can see all of the missing honor or will be able to see all of the missing honors after declarer plays to the first trick. (Play high-low)

(2) YOU will be the first defender to regain the lead and you are planning on returning the suit. (Play high-low).

THE LEAD OF THE JACK

127* In an UNBID or UNSUPPORTED suit, give ATTITUDE. However, if partner can tell that you cannot hold an honor, give COUNT.

(a) **North** (dummy)
Q76

West
J

East (you)
(1) 85
(2) K54

If dummy plays low, play the five, attitude, with both holdings. If dummy plays the queen, play the eight, count, with (1).

(b) **North** (dummy)
AK6

West
J

East (you)
(1) 82
(2) 8532

If dummy wins the trick, play the deuce, attitude; if dummy plays low, give count.

THE LEAD OF THE QUEEN

128. When dummy has the ace-king, give attitude, not count.

(c) **North** (dummy)
AK6

West
Q

East (you)
(1) 84 (4)
(2) 842, 8432 (2)
(3) 1084, 10872 (8)

129. When the three missing honors are either visible in dummy or WILL be visible (if dummy plays low) give count.

North (dummy)
AK10, A10x(x), K10x(x)

West
Q

East (you)
(1) 84 (8)
(2) 842 (2)
(3) 8632 (6)

Not all queen leads are from the queen-jack. If you have the jack, you know partner has led from shortness. If you want the suit continued, signal with an encouraging spot card.

130** If you have SUPPORTED or JUMP SUPPORTED the suit and it is clear (or will be clear after declarer wins the trick),that the opponents have the three outstanding honors (the AK10) give suit preference. THE RULE OF THREE.

North (dummy)
AK10, A10x(x), K10x(x)

West
Q

East (you)
xxx, xxxx
(suit preference)

The Rule of Three also applies when partner leads the jack in a SUPPORTED suit and it is clear (or will be clear after declarer plays), that the opponents have the AKQ of the suit; give suit preference.

131* When dummy has the king and you have the ace, give count, not attitude. A great partner will be able to work out that you have the ace when the queen holds.

North (dummy)
K64

West
Q

East (you)
(1) A82, A9532 (2)
(2) A872 (8)

132. When dummy has worthless cards, third hand gives attitude, not count; overtake with Kx or Ax (usually) and signal positive attitude with 10xx(x) unless you want another suit led.

North (dummy)
873

West	**East**	
Q	(1) 62, 962, 9652	(2)
	(2) K62, 1062	(6)
	(3) K5	(K)
	(4) A5	(A)
	(5) Axx(x)	(?)

With (5) play the ace unless you know it cannot be lost and you are trying to build a later entry to partner's hand.

133. If you know partner's queen lead is from AKQ(x)(x), give count, not attitude. Furthermore, if partner continues the suit, give suit preference with your remaining small cards. When giving count with four, play the jack from J10xx and the ten from 109xx; otherwise second highest.

East-West vul.
Dealer West

North (dummy)
♠ A932
♥ J75
♦ Q2
♣ A876

West
♠ 84
♥ AKQ
♦ J1096
♣ 9532

East (you)
♠ K5
♥ 9862
♦ 8543
♣ KJ10

South
♠ QJ1076
♥ 1043
♦ AK7
♣ Q4

West	**North**	**East**	**South**
Pass	Pass	Pass	1♠
Pass	3♠	All Pass	

Opening lead: ♥Q

At trick one play the ♥8, count. At trick two play the ♥2, suit preference for clubs. If partner shifts to a club after cashing a third heart, declarer winds up losing three hearts, a club, and spade. If partner shifts to the ♦J at trick four, a sharp South will make the hand. As partner's initial pass (has turned up with 10 HCP), marks you with both black kings, declarer can cash the ♠A, strip the diamonds and toss you in with a spade to force a club return.

THE KING FROM KING-QUEEN IN AN UNBID OR UNSUPPORTED SUIT

134* If dummy has small cards, signal attitude; do NOT play high-low with a doubleton; tend to overtake with Ax; signal encouragement with the ace or jack UNLESS you want partner to lead something else.

135** If dummy has the Jxx(x), give COUNT. If the king holds, partner knows you have the ace; if the king loses, partner knows you are giving count with worthless cards.

North (dummy)
J85

East (you)
62, 10632 (6)
A72, A9732 (2)
A2 (?)

Overtake with Ax if you feel you need THREE quick tricks in the suit. If ruffing the third round of the suit will cost you a trump trick or may expose a possible queen of trump in partner's hand, do not overtake.

136** If dummy has Axx(x) and plays low, give attitude; if dummy plays the ace, give count. (If dummy plays the ace, declarer is unlikely to hold the jack).

North (dummy)
A87

West
K

East (you)
(1) 62
(2) J62
(3) J632

With (1) play the deuce if dummy plays low, otherwise the six. With (2) play the six if dummy plays low, otherwise the deuce. With (3) play the six in either case.

137* If dummy has AJx(x), give count regardless. WHEN IT IS CLEAR THAT YOU CANNOT HAVE A MEANINGFUL HONOR, GIVE COUNT.

North (dummy)
AJ76

West
K

East (you)
10532 (5)
1053 (3)
84 (8)

IF PARTNER HAS BID THE SUIT AND LEADS THE KING SHOWING THE KQ.

138* If dummy has Axx(x), give count regardless. Contrast this tip with tip 136.

WHEN PARTNER LEADS THE KING IN A SUIT YOU HAVE BID

139. When partner leads the king in a suit you have bid, give ATTITUDE. Do not woodenly give a positive signal holding the ace; if you want a shift, play low. Partner has to work out what you have in mind by making a quarter turn of the neck to the left to look at the dummy. Note: If your previous bidding has shown a six card suit or longer, your first play is suit preference. (See tip 151)

Neither side vul.
Dealer North

North (dummy)
♠ 9875
♥ J10
♣ KJ6
♣ AQJ10

West
♠ J62
♥ KQ4
♦ 875
♣ K942

East (you)
♠ 43
♥ A8752
♦ AQ103
♣ 63

South
♠ AKQ10
♥ 963
♦ 942
♣ 875

North	**East**	**South**	**West**
1♣	1♥	1♠	2♥
2♠	All Pass		

Opening lead: ♥K

Your first play, attitude, sets the tone for the defense. Play the deuce because you want a shift, a diamond shift. How will partner know? She will use the old neck trick and see all those mean looking clubs and being a genius will deduce you must want a diamond shift. If partner obliges, you can win and underlead your ♥A to partner's known queen. Now a second diamond allows you to win and cash a third. A fourth diamond then promotes the ♠J to the setting trick. Happiness reigns. (At least until the next hand).

THE LEAD OF THE ACE FROM ACE-KING IN AN UNBID OR UNSUPPORTED SUIT

140. Give attitude when partner leads the ace; but there are exceptions. With QJx(x) play the QUEEN promising the jack (or a singleton). Partner can underlead her king if she wishes.

	North (dummy) 753	
West AK86		**East** (you) QJ42 (Q)
	South 109	

141. When dummy has xxx(x) play high-low with a doubleton, but NOT with Qx. (The queen shows the jack). However, if dummy has Jx and you have Qx and can overtrump dummy WITHOUT compromising your trump holding, play the queen. If dummy has Jxx and you have Qx plus worthless trump, and there is some chance that a third trick in the suit can get away if partner does not continue, play the queen. With Qxx(x) signal encouragement if you want the suit continued, NOT simply to show the queen.

	North (dummy) (1) 864 (2) J64	
West A		**East** (you) Q2

If dummy (1) tables, play the deuce; if dummy (2) tables, play the queen if your trump holding will not be weakened by a ruff and there is some chance that a third trick in the suit can go away.

142* When dummy has a doubleton, play high if:

(1) you have a doubleton and can overtrump dummy;
(2) you have a doubleton, cannot overtrump dummy, but may provoke declarer into ruffing higher than necessary.
(3) you have an equal honor— if the signal will not be confused with a doubleton—partner may underlead to your presumed equal honor and wouldn't that be lovely?

North (dummy)
86

West
AK5

East (you)
Q97432

South
J10

Partner leads the ace (or king) in an UNBID suit. You can afford to play the nine— partner will not play you for a doubleton. Had you a doubleton, declarer would have a hidden six card suit!

143* When dummy has J10xx or Jxxx, save your high-lows for doubletons or Qxxx(x) when your second highest card is higher than dummy's second highest card; play low with Qx.

North (dummy)
J854

West
AK6(x)

East (you)
92 (9)
Q72 (2)
Q742 (2)
Q972 (7)

South
103

If you play the seven from Q72 or Q742, partner will continue with the ace thinking you have a doubleton. Instead of you ruffing, declarer will. This in itself is not so terrible; setting up an undeserved winner in dummy is.

144* When dummy has Qxx(x) give count if:

(1) Partner or dummy has bid the suit or
(2) Declarer has bid two other suits or
(3) You have a doubleton or
(4) The opponents are at the five level or higher.

If none of these conditions exist, play low.

145* When dummy has KQx(x), give count. But if you have raised the suit, partner knows that declarer is short, so give suit preference. (See tip 152).

146. When partner's lead shows AK doubleton, give suit preference on the lead of the SECOND honor (you don't know it is AK doubleton until you see the second honor).

Both vul.
Dealer South

North (dummy)
♠ QJ65
♥ 103
♦ KQ98
♣ 1072

West
♠ AK
♥ J96
♦ 10753
♣ 9653

East (you)
♠ 109832
♥ 5
♦ AJ4
♣ KJ84

South
♠ 74
♥ AKQ8742
♦ 65
♣ AQ

South	**West**	**North**	**East**
1♥	Pass	1♠	Pass
4♥	All Pass		

Opening lead: ♠ K

Your first play is count (see tip 144) your second, suit preference. At trick two play the ♠10 to show diamond strength. Partner's diamond return followed by a third spade promotes the ♥J to the setting trick.

Now the other side of the coin: when you have two honors doubleton in the suit partner has led and you cash both of them, partner's second play in the suit is suit preference telling you what to lead to get your ruff.

Neither side vul.
Dealer South

North (dummy)
♠ KJ83
♥ K54
♦ 753
♣ 864

East (you)
♠ 72
♥ AQ
♦ J1094
♣ 107532

South	**West**	**North**	**East**
1♠	Pass	1♠	Pass
4♠	All Pass		

Opening lead: ♥J

Dummy plays low and you win the first two tricks with the queen and ace, declarer playing the six and eight, partner the three. What do you play at trick three?

A club. Partner has spoken. That ♥3 says lead a club. Unless you have a very good reason, DON'T CROSS PARTNER'S INTENTIONS!

Declarer's hand: ♠ AQ10965 ♥ 862 ♦ AKQ ♣ K
Partner's hand: ♠ 4 ♥ J10973 ♦ 862 ♣ AQJ9

A club shift followed by a heart return is the only defense to defeat this contract.

147. Sometimes you must play an encouraging card from worthless holdings. You do this for fear partner's second winner may vanish unless cashed at once.

Neither side vul.
Dealer South

North (dummy)
♠ J4
♥ Q98
♦ AQ98
♣ AQ105

East (you)
♠ AK
♥ 76432
♦ 764
♣ 862

South	**West**	**North**	**East**
3♠	Pass	4♠	All Pass

Opening lead: ♥A (Which heart do you play?)

You can "see" that there are no tricks coming from the minors, but partner can't. Worse, if partner's doesn't cash a second heart it will surely be lost on one of the minors. Therefore, you should play a high heart at trick one to encourage partner to try to cash a second heart winner. Even if it gets ruffed, nothing has been lost. Once again the answer to an accurate signal is to first consider the hand as a unit rather than zero in blindly on your holding in partner's suit.

Declarer's hand: ♠ Q1098732 ♥ J10 ♦K3 ♣ K3
Partner's hand: ♠65 ♥ AK5 ♦ J1052 ♣ J974

148** A trick one signal that requires a mature relationship with partner is the play of a CRAZY HONOR CARD in an unbid suit (that cannot be a doubleton) asking partner to shift to the ILLOGICAL suit (dummy's stronger suit). If you want a shift to the logical suit (dummy's shorter side suit), play low.

East-West vul.
Dealer North

North (dummy)
♠ Q54
♥ J1084
♦ 103
♣ AK109

East (you)
♠ J9762
♥ A6
♦ J6542
♣ 6

North	East	South	West
Pass	Pass	1♥	Pass
3♥	Pass	4♥	Pass
Pass	Pass		

Opening lead: ♠ A Which spade do you play?

Play the ♠J to ask for the illogical shift, a club. The idea is to win the first trump play, put partner in with a spade and get a club ruff. LOOK AHEAD.

Note* This crazy honor card cannot be the king. The play of king under the ace shows solidity and asks for a continuation. (Unless dummy has a singleton, in which case it is suit preference).

South's hand: ♠ 83 ♥ KQ953 ♦ AK ♣ QJ74
Partner's hand: ♠ AK10 ♥ 72 ♦ Q987 ♣ 8532

THE LEAD OF THE KING FROM ACE-KING IN A SUPPORTED SUIT

149. When partner leads the king in a supported suit, give attitude. Nine times out of ten a positive signal shows the queen; opener can underlead the ace if desperate.

Neither side vul.
Dealer West

North (dummy)
♠ 76
♥ KQ75
♦ 987
♣ AKJ10

West
♠ AKJ32
♥ 42
♦ A102
♣ 763

East (you)
♠ Q94
♥ 86
♦ QJ653
♣ 984

South
♠ 1085
♥ AJ1093
♦ K4
♣ Q52

West	**North**	**East**	**South**
1♠	Dbl.	2♠	4♥
All Pass			

Opening lead: ♠K

Play the ♠9 at trick one at once showing the queen and telling partner not to shift to the logical suit, diamonds. If partner pays dummy's club suit the proper respect, partner will lead a low spade at trick two allowing you to shift to the ♦Q. Against this Herculean defense, declarer loses the first four tricks.

150** If dummy has Qx(x) and you have given a simple, (as opposed to a jump) raise, give count.

(a)

North (dummy)
Q98

West
K

East (you)
1043, 10432 (give count)

However, if dummy has Qxx(x) and the bidding has marked declarer with a singleton or void, give suit preference.

(b)

North (dummy)
Q864

West
AK1032

East (you)
J95, J975

Assuming you have raised or jump raised a known five card suit or even jump raised a four card suit, declarer is known to have a singleton at MOST. In any case, partner is not going to be interested in continuing the suit, so give suit preference.

Dealer South
North-South vul.

North (dummy).
♠ Q74
♥ Q106
♦ 732
♣ A1075

East (you)
♠ J862
♥ 42
♦ KJ65
♣ 864

South	**West**	**North**	**East**
1♥	1♠	2♥	3♠*
4♥	All Pass		

* Preemptive (no kidding)

Opening lead: ♠K Which spade do you play at trick one?

Play the ♠J, suit preference for diamonds. Now all partner has to do is remember the tip and lead a low diamond.

Declarer's hand: ♠ 9 ♥ AKJ975 ♦ Q98 ♣ KQJ
Partner's hand: ♠ AK1053 ♥ 83 ♦ A104 ♣ 763

A low diamond switch at trick allows your side to win the first four tricks, three diamonds and a spade.

WHEN TO GIVE SUIT PREFERENCE (A DANGEROUS TOPIC!)

151** If your bidding has promised a SIX card or longer suit give suit preference at trick one. (Even if dummy wins the trick).

North (dummy)
J104

West
A

East (you)
KQ9732

Partner leads the ace of your preempted suit. If you want a continuation (most likely), play THIRD lowest, the seven. By withholding TWO lower cards, partner is supposed to assume a continuation is desired. If you want a shift to the lower ranking side suit, play your lowest, card, the deuce. If you want a shift to the higher ranking side suit, play the highest card you can AFFORD (other than the king which asks for a continuation), the NINE.

152* When partner leads the ace of a SUPPORTED suit and dummy comes down with KQx(x) or stronger, give suit preference.

North (dummy)
♥ KQ84

West
♥ A10732

East (you)
♥ J65

South
♥ 9

Spades are trump, you have supported hearts,and partner leads the ace. Give suit preference. The ♥J asks for a diamond shift, the ♥5, a club shift. The ♥6 is neutral announcing equal strength in the minors.

153** When partner leads a card that is about to take a trick and dummy has a singleton, give suit preference but only if you have bid or JUMP supported the suit; otherwise give ATTITUDE.

Neither side vul.
Dealer South

North (dummy)
♠ AJ108
♥ 3
♦ J873
♣ K974

West
♠ 632
♥ A942
♦ 5
♣ Q10832

East (you)
♠ KQ9
♥ KJ10865
♦ 62
♣ J5

South
♠ 754
♥ Q7
♦ AKQ1094
♣ A6

South	West	North	East
1♦	Pass	1♠	2♥
3♦	4♥	5♦	All Pass

Opening lead: ♥A

Play the ♥J, suit preference for spades. If partner shifts to a spade at trick two, declarer cannot strip the hand and endplay you.

WHEN TO SIGNAL ATTITUDE

154** You may want to encourage partner for a number of reasons:
(1) You want the suit continued because you are strong in the suit.
(2) You have nothing else and you feel a shift may be disastrous.
(3) When dummy has a singleton and you have neither bid nor jump supported the suit.

Conversely you may wish to give a negative attitude signal when:

(1) You are weak in the suit.
(2) You are strong in the suit but prefer partner leads another suit.

In short, your attitude not only depends upon your holding in the suit partner has led, but your feeling about the hand as a whole.

155** When partner leads a winner and dummy has a singleton, give ATTITUDE unless you have bid or jump supported the suit. (See previous tip.)

East-West vul.
Dealer South

North (dummy)
♠ AK2
♥ 8
♦ J1083
♣ KQ1092

East (you)
♠ J865
♥ K742
♦ KQ9
♣ 83

South	West	North	East
1♠	Pass	2♣	Pass
2♠	Pass	4♥*	Pass
4NT**	Pass	5♥***	Pass
6♠	All Pass		

* Splinter
** Key Card Blackwood
*** Two key cards (including the trump king)

Opening lead: ♥A Which heart do you play?

Play the ♥7 to ask for a continuation. Once dummy trumps, you have a trump trick. Had you wanted a diamond shift, the logical suit, you should play a low heart; had you wanted a club shift, the illogical suit, play the ♥K. (The play of the king under the ace normally shows solidity and asks for a continuation. However when dummy has a SINGLETON, it is a suit preference play).

Declarer's hand: ♠ Q109743 ♥ Q103 ♦ A7 ♣ AJ
Partner's hand: ♠ - ♥ AJ965 ♦ 6542 ♣ 7654

156* Holding an equal honor to the card partner leads is NOT reason enough to give an encouraging signal. You must want that suit continued. If you don't, give a discouraging signal. A biggie.

East-West vul.
Dealer South

North (dummy)
♠ 105
♥ 93
♦ KQ1076
♣ QJ64

West (you)
♠ J32
♥ Q2
♦ 743
♣ K9873

South	West	North	East
1♠	Pass	1NT	3♥*
4♠	All Pass		

* Intermediate

Opening lead: ♥Q

Partner overtakes with the king, cashes the ♥J, and plunks down the ♣A, declarer following. Your play?

Play your most discouraging club. Although your ♣K MAY take the setting trick (if declarer has another club), your ♠J is SURE to take the setting trick if partner plays a third heart.

WHEN TO GIVE COUNT

157. When partner leads low and dummy plays a card which you cannot top (a queen or lower), give count.

(a)

North (dummy)
AJ10

West
3

East (you)
86 (8)
854 (4)
8542 (5)

When the play from dummy marks you with a particular honor, give count.

(b)

North (dummy)
AJ5

West
K10643

East (you)
(a) Q92 (2)
(b) Q972 (9)

South
(a) 87
(b) 8

Partner leads the four and dummy plays the ace. It should be clear to you that partner has the king and it should be clear to partner that you have the queen, so give count.

(c)

North (dummy)
AQ5

West
K1063

East (you)
J72 (2)
J972 (9)

South
984
84

Partner leads low and dummy plays the queen. Partner knows that if declarer had the jack, she would have played low from dummy. Her play marks you with the jack, so give count.

158* With worthless cards that cannot possibly drive out anything worthwhile, give count; do NOT play third hand high.

North (dummy)
AJ6

West
K1083

East (you)
752 (2)

South
Q94

If partner leads the three and dummy plays the six, play the deuce, count. Do not play the seven, it will be interpreted as a count card.

GIVING PRESENT COUNT (THE SECOND PLAY IN THE SUIT)

159** When RETURNING partner's suit give present count.

North (dummy)
95

West
2

East (you)
A83 (8)
A843 (3)
A8743 (8)
AJ8743 (3)

Consider each of your holdings WITHOUT the ace and assume an OPPONENT is leading the suit and you want to give count. You give present count with what you have left. With 83 play the eight, and with 843 play the three, etc.

When your first play in a suit is attitude, your second play is present count.

North (dummy)
K107

West
A4

East (you)
(1) QJ8532 (8) (2)
(2) QJ852 (8) (5)

South
(1) 96
(2) 963

Partner leads the ace and you signal encouragement with the eight When partner continues the suit to dummy's king, give PRESENT COUNT. See previous tip.

160* When your first play in a suit is count, your next play is suit preference.

North (dummy)
QJ7

West
AK853

East (you)
942

South
106

Partner leads the ace of an unsupported suit and you play the deuce, count. Your next play in the suit, regardless who leads it, is suit preference.

WHEN PARTNER LEADS A TRUMP

161* When partner leads a trump from known weakness and catches you with a trump honor, play low if you must conserve your trump honor to kill a dummy entry.

Both sides vul.
Dealer South

North (dummy)
♠ 962
♥ KQJ65
♦ 53
♣ J109

West
♠ 54
♥ 973
♦ Q8764
♣ K87

East (you)
♠ 1073
♥ 10842
♦ 109
♣ Q432

South
♠ AKQJ8
♥ A
♦ AKJ2
♣ A65

South	West	North	East
2♣	Pass	2♥	Pass
2♠	Pass	3♠	Pass
6♠	All Pass		

Opening lead: ♠4

This slam is on your head at trick one! You must conserve your ♠10. If you squander it at trick one, declarer can cash the ♥A and draw trump ENDING IN DUMMY and wind up with 13 tricks. If you play low at trick one, declarer may wind up with nine!

162. When partner leads a trump from known weakness and catches you with an honor that could become a trick if dummy trumps once or twice, play low.

Neither side vul.
Dealer East

North (dummy)
♠ 9
♥ Q1087632
♦ A54
♣ 76

West
♠ Q72
♥ AJ94
♦ 32
♣ 10542

East (you)
♠ KJ1083
♥ K5
♦ Q76
♣ K93

South
♠ A654
♥ -
♦ KJ1098
♣ AQJ8

East	South	West	North
1♠	2♦	2♠	3♥
Pass	4♣	Pass	4♦
Pass	5♦	All Pass	

Opening lead: ♦2

Partner, having dummy's long side suit locked up, leads a trump. When dummy plays low, your play to this trick decides the outcome of the contract. If you play the queen, declarer can come to eleven tricks via five diamonds in the closed hand, the ♠A, two spade ruffs in dummy and three clubs. If you play low, you will eventually make a trump trick (to go along with a club and a spade). (After declarer ruffs two spades in dummy, your ♦Q stands up.

163. When partner leads a trump from known weakness and catches you with a trump honor that can later be used to overtrump dummy, play low.

164. When partner leads a trump and finds you with QJx or KJx and dummy has small cards, your best bet to make declarer think the honors are split is to play the queen from QJx, and the jack from KJx.

SHORT SUIT LEADS

165* When partner leads a known singleton and you have worthless cards in the suit, give suit preference.

Both sides vul. **Dealer South**	**North** (dummy) ♠ QJ65 ♥ KQJ8 ♦ Q8 ♣ J54	
West ♠ A92 ♥ 5 ♦ K10765 ♣ 10986		**East** (you) ♠ 74 ♥ 97432 ♦ A432 ♣ 32
	South ♠ K1083 ♥ A106 ♦ J9 ♣ AKQ7	

South	West	North	East
1NT	Pass	2♣	Pass
2♠	Pass	4♠	All Pass

Opening lead: ♥5

Partner's lead must be a singleton, so play the ♥9, suit preference to show diamond interest. After this signal, the defense is easy. Partner wins the ♠A, leads a diamond to your ace, ruffs the heart return and cashes the ♦K. One in the soup.

166* In order to determine whether partner's lead is a singleton or a doubleton, use the old "singleton assumption" test. For the moment assume the lead is a singleton, and then ask yourself if declarer's presumed length is consistent with the bidding. If it isn't, play partner for a doubleton.

Neither side vul.	**North** (dummy)	
Dealer South	♠ J109	
	♥ 108542	
	♦ 2	
	♣ A876	
		East (you)
		♠ A762
		♥ -
		♦ KQ853
		♣ KJ92

South	**West**	**North**	**East**
1♥	Pass	4♥	Dbl.
All Pass			

Opening lead: ♠8 Plan your defense.

Partner's lead must be a doubleton. If a singleton, declarer has five spades. Unlikely. Play partner for a doubleton spade and signal encouragement to keep the lines of communications open. When partner wins a hoped for trump trick, partner can return her remaining spade and secure a ruff.

Declarer's hand: ♠ KQ53 ♥ KJ1097 ♦ AJ10 ♣ Q
Partner's hand: ♠ 84 ♥ AQ3 ♦ 9764 ♣ 10543

167. Holding the ace of partner's short suit lead plus an outside ace, no need to worry whether the lead is a singleton or a doubleton. Win the lead and give a suit preference return. If partner ruffs, great; if not, partner knows how to put you in for a later ruff.

OVERTAKING PARTNER'S LEAD

168. To determine whether you can afford to overtake, use your old friend the "singleton assumption" test. Assume the lead is a singleton and ask yourself if your spot cards are strong enough to overtake without setting up an extra trick for declarer. If the answer is yes, overtake; if the answer is no, don't.

	North (dummy)	
	976	
West		**East** (you)
J		(1) KQ1082
		(2) KQ1032
	South	
	(1) A543	
	(2) A854	

With (1) you can afford to overtake; with (2) you cannot; declarer's fourth highest card is higher than your fourth highest card.

SIGNALING REVIEW

A. WHEN TO GIVE POSITIVE ATTITUDE:

1. When partner leads an honor and dummy has worthless cards.
2. When partner's lead is taken in dummy with the ace or king and you want the suit continued.
3. When partner leads an honor in a suit you have bid, (not having promised a six card suit).
4. When partner leads a winner in a suit you have neither bid nor jump supported, and dummy has a singleton.
5. During the course of play when partner leads a high honor.

B. WHEN TO GIVE COUNT:

1. Partner leads low, dummy plays the queen or lower, and you can't beat dummy's card.
2. Partner leads the ace in a bid suit that you have NOT supported and dummy tables with KQx(x).
3. Partner leads the Ace (from AK(x) and dummy has Qx(x)(x) if:
   (1) you have supported the suit.
   (2) partner or dummy has bid the suit
   (3) declarer has bid two other suits.
   (4) the opponents are at the five level or higher.
4. Partner leads the K from a KQ combination in an unbid or unsupported suit and dummy has AJx(x).
5. When dummy's honor holding or the eventual play to the first trick will mark you with the missing honor.
6. When dummy's holding or the eventual play to the first trick will mark you with no honor.
7. With a doubleton in an ATTITUDE situation when YOU will be next on lead and are planning to return the suit.
8. When partner leads the Q from a suspected AKQ combination-presuming you use this convention.
9. Partner leads low and you have worthless cards.
10. Partner leads the king, dummy has Axx(x) and plays the ace.
11. Partner leads the queen, dummy has the king, you have the ace, and dummy plays low.

C. WHEN TO GIVE SUIT PREFERENCE:

1. Partner leads your known six card suit (or longer).

2. Partner leads the ace of a SUPPORTED suit and dummy has KQx(x).

3** Partner leads the K from a KQ combination in a SUPPORTED suit and dummy has AJx(x).

4. Partner leads the K from an AK combination in a supported suit, dummy has Qxx(x) and declarer is KNOWN to have a singleton or void.

5. You think you may be giving partner a ruff.

6. When dummy has a singleton and you have bid or jump supported the suit that has been led.

7. The opponents have the first three tricks in a suit you have supported.

(5)
THIRD HAND PLAY VS. NOTRUMP

Third hand play vs. notrump is a bit less complicated than third hand vs. suit: (1) partner usually leads from length; (2) giving or getting a ruff is no longer a concern; (3) most signals are attitude as opposed to count or suit preference. (4) over-taking, unblocking and keeping the lines of communication open are also vital concerns.

PARTNER LEADS LOW—PRESUMABLY FOURTH BEST—THE RULE OF ELEVEN

169. Apply the rule of 11 when partner leads what appears to be a fourth highest card.

Both sides vul.
Dealer South

North (dummy)
♠ 98
♥ J1098
♦ KQ4
♣ KJ32

East (you)
♠ Q103
♥ A75
♦ 9832
♣ 954

South	**West**	**North**	**East**
1NT*	Pass	2♣	Pass
2♦	Pass	3NT	All Pass

*16-18

Opening lead: ♠6

Your queen fetches declarer's king. At trick two declarer crosses to the ♦Q, partner playing the five, and leads the ♥J intending to finesse. Up or down Mrs. Brown?

Don't tell me you went for that finesse bit! If you use the "rule" you know that partner's spades are now solid as declarer only started with one spade higher than the six. In addition, you know from the bidding that partner has at least five spades. Don't let declarer steal the contract from under your nose. Win that ♥A and take your winning spades.

Declarer's hand: ♠ K54 ♥ KQ4 ♦ A105 ♣ AQ87
Partner's hand: ♠ AJ762 ♥ 632 ♦ J76 ♣ 106

Note: When partner is known to have a four card suit (because you can see all of the lower cards), there is no need to apply the rule. (You know how many cards declarer has and all of them will be higher than the one partner has led).

(a)

North (dummy)
K53

West
Q1087

East (you)
AJ92

South
64

When partner leads the seven and dummy plays low, the rule tells you that declarer has no card higher than the seven so play the two and allow partner to win the trick. (However if partner has decided to lead the seven from Q87, and declarer wins the first trick with the ten, I don't know you; I've never known you; and don't say hello).

(b)

North (dummy)
AQ8

West
6

East (you)
K102 (10)
K92 (9)
K9 (9)

South
xx, xxx or xxxx

In each case the rule tells you that declarer has no card higher than the six. Therefore, if dummy plays low, take the trick with your second highest card...nonchalantly with K9 doubleton, please.

170. When the "rule" doesn't work, it hasn't been repealed; partner has doublecrossed you and not led fourth best.

North (dummy)
AJ10

West
7

East (you)
Q5

Dummy plays the ten and your queen loses to the king. Partner has not led fourth best. (The "rule" tells you that declarer has no card higher than the seven). Time to readjust one's thinking. Partner may have started with 7xx(x) or 97xx.

SPECIALIZED THIRD HAND PLAYS

171* When partner leads a suit that DECLARER has bid, the presumption is that partner is quite strong in the suit. Do not expect partner to give honest count; just return the suit. Partner may decide to lead fifth best from something like KJ972 in order not to waste a valuable spot card if declarer also has five cards in the suit.

172. Do not be a slave to third hand high. Do not play third hand high with AQx. It is usually right to play the queen.

North (dummy)
8

West
J9532

East (you)
AQ6 (Q)

South
K1074

Assuming the queen drives out the king, communication between the partnership remains intact. The defense has far less flexibility if the ace is played prematurely.

Play the same with AJx or KJx but ONLY if you have the important outside entry, partner has led from a five card suit, minimum, and you will still have enough tricks to defeat the contract after declarer wins the opening lead. In other words, you have to know what you are doing.

North
A2

West
108743

East (you)
KJ5

South
Q96

A variation on a theme. When partner leads low and dummy plays low, play the jack. If the jack wins, return the king to unblock the suit. If the jack loses, play the king next. You are playing partner for either the ten or the queen and your play allows the partnership to establish the suit even though partner may not have an outside entry.

173. Do not play third hand high if dummy's holding is so strong that the play will cost you a trick.

North (dummy)
QJ92

West
103

East (you)
K7654

South
A8

When partner leads the ten and dummy plays the jack, only play the king against your future mother-in-law — and even then, only if you want her to tell her son to cancel the engagement.

174. Do not play third hand high with 9xxxx, 10xxxx, Jxxxx or Qxxxx if your play is likely to block the suit.

(a)

North (dummy)
1098

West
A62

East (you)
J7543

South
KQ

When **West** leads low play the three, count. It can't be right to play the jack. Play the same with Qxxxx or even Kxxxx.

(b)

North (dummy)
4

West
Q1082

East (you)
97653

South
AKJ

When partner leads low, play the three, count. The nine cannot possibly drive out anything worthwhile, but it can, and will, block the suit.

WHEN PARTNER LEADS YOUR SUIT (WILL WONDERS NEVER CEASE)

175. If declarer has only one stopper, try to remove that stopper while partner still remains with at least one card in your suit.

(a)

North (dummy)
87

West
1042

East (you)
AQJ93 (J)

South
K65

When partner leads low showing three (or four) cards in the suit, play the jack. If South refuses, continue with a low card to drive out the king. Playing the ace prematurely allows the declarer to hold up until the third round.

(b) **North** (dummy)
J104

West
83

East (you)
AK972

South
Q65

When partner leads the eight, and you have no certain outside entry, signal encouragement; do not play an honor. The opponents are entitled to one trick, let them have it early, partner retaining one card in the suit.

176. If the opponents are entitled to TWO tricks in your long suit and partner has a doubleton, allow the opponents to win the first trick; if partner has three cards, allow the opponents to win the first two tricks in the suit. In both cases, partner retains one card in your suit.

(a) **North** (dummy)
753

West
82

East (you)
AJ1064

South
KQ9

Play the ten at trick one. If you and a partner each have a side entry, and partner can use hers first, this suit can be established and run.

(b) **North** (dummy)
96

West
J108

East (you)
A7432 (7)

South
KQ5

Assuming the position is clear (jack denies or declarer's bidding has shown a double stopper), it is better to concede the first two tricks retaining one card in partner's hand in case you have no outside entry but partner does. If you duck the first two rounds and declarer turns up with KQ doubleton, this tip was a misprint.

WHEN DUMMY HAS AN HONOR AND YOU HAVE A HIGHER HONOR AND DUMMY PLAYS LOW

177. When there is an honor in dummy and you have a HIGHER honor tend to conserve your honor if dummy plays low. However, if you don't play your honor, the card you play must be the equivalent of the nine or higher; if it isn't, play your honor.

North (dummy)
J65

West
2

East (you)
K943 (9)
K83 (K)
K98 (8)
Q97 (9)
A94 (A) (the exception)

The major exception is playing the ace from A9x(x) when dummy has the jack; play the 10 from A10x, declarer may have Kxx and the play of the ten will discourage a holdup play.

WHEN DUMMY HAS AN HONOR AND IT IS HIGHER THAN YOURS

178. When dummy has the higher honor, and dummy plays LOW, play third hand as if dummy had small cards.

(a)

North (dummy)
A65

West
2

East (you)
Q103 (Q)
QJ3 (J)

(b)

North (dummy)
A85

West
93

East (you)
KJ742

South
Q106

The exception. If you are trying to establish your suit and you have only one outside entry, it may be important to allow partner to keep her remaining card. If partner has an early entry and you have a later entry, the suit can be established if you do not win the first trick; signal encouragement instead.

WHEN PARTNER LEADS AN HONOR

In order to discuss third hand play when partner leads an honor (presumably from length), you must have agreements on the meaning of each honor card lead.

HONOR LEADS —THE TEN

179. If the lead of the ten can be from interior sequences such A109, K109 or Q109 as well as top of a sequence (standard), and dummy has worthless cards, play high.

	North (dummy) 63	
West 10		**East** (you) K72
	South ?	

Play the king; partner may have led from the Q109(x) or A109x(x)(x). The bad news is that if the king loses you still won't know what partner has led from.

If you play the lead of the ten shows either top of a sequence or AJ10(x), play the king. At least if it loses you know that declarer remains with the queen and the jack.

HONOR LEADS — THE JACK

180. Playing standard leads, the jack is either top of a sequence or KJ10(x)(x), AJ10(x)(x).In order to be safe, play third hand high holding the king or the ace. If you play "jack denies", you know declarer's honor holding, and it may not be necessary to play third hand high.

	North (dummy) 53	
West J10864		**East** (you) K72
	South AQ9	

Here the play of the king is wasteful, but necessary if you fear partner may have AJ10(x)(x). If you KNOW that declarer has both the ace and the queen, you can signal encouragement allowing partner to continue the suit safely.

HONOR LEADS —THE QUEEN

181. When partner leads the queen, assume it's top of a sequence and:
(1) Signal encouragement if you have the ace, king or ten.
(2) Signal encouragement if you have the nine and dummy has the singleton ace or king.
(3) Unblock with 10x, Kx or Ax.
(4) Unblock the jack if you lead the Q from KQ109(x).
(5) Give count if partner will be able to tell that you can't possibly have an honor (ten or higher).

HONOR LEADS —THE KING

182. When partner leads the king, assume top of a sequence and: (1) Signal encouragement with any honor. (2) Unblock with honor doubleton. ** (3) Play the ten from 109x when dummy has a singleton or small doubleton (4) Play small with two, three or four worthless cards.

	North (dummy)	
	74	
West		**East** (you)
KQJ3		1092
	South	
	A865	

Play the ten under the king to show the nine. If the king holds, partner can lead low to unblock the suit. However, if you want partner to lead something else, play low from 109x.

HONOR LEADS —THE ACE

183. The lead of the ace, the strongest lead, shows a powerful holding missing one of the top four honors: AKQ10(x), AKJ10(x) or AQJ10(x). You should:
(1) Unblock the missing honor if you have it.
(2) Give count if you don't.

	North (dummy)		
	73		
West		**East**	
A		84	(8)
		842	(2)
		8642	(6)
		J86	(J)
		Q942	(Q)

WHEN TO GIVE COUNT

184. Give count when partner leads low and dummy plays the queen (or a lower card) which you cannot top.

West	North (dummy)	East	
	North (dummy) QJ10		
West K8632		**East** 94 954	 (9) (4)
	South A75 A7		

Your count play at trick one tells partner whether it is safe to continue the suit.

185. Give count when partner leads the jack, queen or ace and it is clear that you cannot have an honor.

West	North (dummy)	East	
	North (dummy) A106		
West QJ975		**East** (you) 82 832	 (8) (2)
	South K43 K4		

If partner leads the queen and dummy plays low, give count. Declarer is about to win the king and partner will know that you cannot possibly have an honor.

186* Give count when partner leads low, dummy plays low, and you have worthless cards in the suit. Do NOT play third hand high. A "worthless" card at notrump is defined as an eight or lower; play the same vs. a suit contract.

West	North (dummy)	East	
	North (dummy) A107		
West 4		**East** (you) 82 832 8632	 (8) (2) (6)

If dummy plays low, play the card in parenthesis.

THE PLAY WITH EQUAL HONORS

187* Play equal honors out of order as a request for partner to unblock her highest remaining card.

(a)

	North (dummy)	
	76	
West		**East** (you)
Q82		AKJ93
	South	
	1054	

When partner leads the deuce, play the ace and then the king asking partner to unblock the queen.

(b)

	North (dummy)	
	J10	
West		**East** (you)
932		KQ865
	South	
	A74	

When partner leads low, play the king. Assuming this holds, return the queen to ask partner to unblock the nine. (If partner has Axx and declarer 9xx, burn the book).

188* Holding equal honors, play the highest equal if dummy wins the trick, but not if it can cost a trick.

(a)

	North (dummy)	
	A8	
West		**East**
54		(1) QJ1097 (Q) (2) QJ1062 (6)
	South	
	(1) K632 (2) K973	

Partner leads the five and dummy plays the ace. With (1) you can afford to play the queen; with (2) you cannot.

(b)

	North (dummy)	
	A2	
West		**East** (you)
J10974		KQ3
	South	
	865	

Partner leads the jack and dummy plays the ace; unblock with the KING. (Always unblock with the HIGHER equal.) If dummy plays low, win the queen and return the king. Winning with the king and returning the queen shows a doubleton. (See tip 125.)

189. When partner leads a suit in which you have a sequence and dummy plays low, play your lowest equal first, your highest equal next. If dummy wins the trick, play your highest equal.

North (dummy)
A74

West
53

East (you)
J10982

South
KQ6

When partner leads the five and dummy plays low, play the eight and the jack next. If dummy wins the ace, play the jack.

190. With two equal honors doubleton (J10), (QJ), (KQ) (AK), play the higher equal if either you or dummy wins the trick. If you cannot be sure you are going to win the trick, play your lower equal.

North (dummy)
A65

West
4

East (you)
QJ

If dummy plays the ace, play the queen; if dummy plays low, play the jack.

RETURNING PARTNER'S SUIT

191* With two cards remaining return the higher; with three cards remaining return the lowest unless:

(1) Declarer is known to have started with four cards in which case return your highest card if it is a nine, ten or jack.

(2) Partner may have greater length than you and your high intermediates may block the suit. If this possibility exists, return the HIGHER of two intermediates.

(a)

North (dummy)
9

West
K1082

East (you)
AJ53

South
Q764

Win the ace and return the jack; declarer is marked with four cards.

(b) **North** (dummy)
42

West
A8765

East (you)
KJ103

South
Q9

Win the king and return the jack to begin an unblock.

(c) **North** (dummy)
98

West
Q6432

East (you)
K1075

South
AJ

Partner leads the three to the king and ace. Later, return the ten to unblock the suit.

192** When partner leads low and dummy has worthless cards and you have AJ109(x) or A1098(x), win the ace and return your original fourth highest card. As long as you and partner are on the same wavelength, partner will have an easier time working out this ambiguous position.

(a) **North** (dummy)
86

West
K5432

East (you)
AJ109

South
Q7

Win the ace and return the nine. Partner will have to work out whether you started with A9 or AJ109. If you return the jack, partner, with no side entry, may duck the second round playing you for AJx and declarer for Q10x. If you return the nine, partner will have no reason to duck.

(b) **North** (dummy)
63

West
KQ542

East (you)
A1098

South
J7

Win the ace and return the eight. It is your best chance to run the suit. Partner will play you for A8 or A1098. In either case, it is safe for partner to win and return a low card. If you return the ten, partner is very likely to block the suit by winning the queen and continuing with the king.

193. When dummy has a doubleton and partner and you each have four cards, return your lowest card.

North (dummy)
75

West
A932

East (you)
KJ64

South
Q108

Win the king and return the four. No need to return high when declarer has three cards, only when she has four. See tip 191.

194** With a five card suit, return the highest spot card you can afford without blocking the suit. Partner can work out from the bidding and the spots whether you started with three or five cards.

North (dummy)
10

West
AJ95

East (you)
K8732

South
Q64

Win the king and return the eight showing three or five cards originally. If you return the more conventional three, partner will not be able to tell whether you started with four or five cards. A TWO card differential is easier to deal with.

195** Holding known length, return your lowest card with a six card suit. Using this method, the return of a low card shows an original holding of four or six cards.

North (dummy)
7

West (you)
J95

East
A108632

South
KQ4

You lead low in partner's overcalled suit. Partner wins and returns the DEUCE showing four or six. Assume six because of the overcall, etc. If partner returns the six, original fourth best, it is not immediately clear whether partner started with a five or a six card suit.

** The opening leader can also lead fourth best and then play UP the line to show a four or six card suit.

North (dummy)
8

West (you)
J97654

East
A2

South
KQ103

You lead the six to the eight, ace and three. When partner returns the deuce and declarer plays the king, play the seven to show an original holding of four or six cards. Using this method, third hand can infer that the opening leader has exactly a five card suit when she plays a lower card than the one that she has led.

CARD COMBINATIONS

196. Holding a side entry plus honor doubleton in the suit partner has led, unblock your honor if dummy wins the trick.

North (dummy)
K4

West
A108632

East (you)
J5 (unblock the J under the K)

South
Q97

197* If partner leads low and dummy has Jx or Qx and dummy plays low, play third hand high with A10xx(x) or K10xx(x).

North (dummy)
Q7

West
A8632

East (you)
K1054 (K)

South
J9

If declarer had the ace, she would have played the queen from dummy.

198* When partner leads low and dummy has small cards, play the JACK from QJ10(x) and the TEN from J109(x).

(a)

North (dummy)
43

West
A9762

East (you)
QJ10 (J)

South
K85

If you play the ten and it loses to the king, partner may fear you have J10x, declarer KQx, and not return the suit. If you play the jack, partner will be forced to play you for QJx or Jxx. In either case it is safe for partner to return the suit.

(b)

	North (dummy)	
	43	
West		**East** (you)
K8762		J109 (10)
	South	
	AQ5	

If you play the nine, partner may fear you have 109x, declarer AQJ, and not return the suit. If you play the ten, partner will play you for 10x or J10x. In either case partner can afford to return the suit without losing a trick.

199* When signaling attitude with equal spot cards, signal with the higher equal.

	North (dummy)	
	5	
West		**East** (you)
QJ4		A9872
	South	
	K1063	

When partner leads the queen, signal with the nine denying the ten.

200* When dummy has 10x or Jx and you have Q8x, Q9x, K8x, K9x or A9x, and dummy plays low, play your middle card if declarer is KNOWN to have a FOUR card suit. If you cannot be sure, play third hand high.

	North (dummy)	
	105	
West		**East**
A832		K97
	South	
	QJ64	

When partner leads the deuce and dummy plays low, play the nine as declarer is known to have four cards. The play of the nine holds declarer to one trick; the play of the king cedes two.

MISCELLANEOUS

201. To help you determine partner's length when a low card is led, look for the LOWER missing spot cards. If there are none, assume a four card suit.

North (dummy)
J73

West
4

East (you)
(1) K102
(2) K105

In (1) both the deuce and trey are visible, so assume partner has a four card suit; in (2) the deuce is missing so the count is not clear until that card appears. (Strong declarers conceal the lower spot cards as long as possible).

202. Suit preference is a rare bird at trick one. However, if partner leads dummy's solid suit, give suit preference, your attitude is known from coast to coast.

North (dummy)
AKQJ

West
86

East (you)
10732 (give suit preference)

South
954

203* With a powerful unbid suit, drastic measures may be in order to attract partner's attention. What you must NOT do is make an ambiguous play in the suit partner has led.

Neither side vul.
Dealer South

North (dummy)
♠ Q85
♥ Q83
♦ KQJ10
♣ 432

West
♠ J9763
♥ 954
♦ A6
♣ 1096

East (you)
♠ 102
♥ AKJ10
♦ 9752
♣ J75

South
♠ AK7
♥ 762
♦ 843
♣ AKQ8

South	West	North	East
1NT	Pass	3NT	All Pass

Opening lead: ♠6

Once you see dummy, your main concern is to get partner to shift to a heart (without beating on your chest), but how? Start by playing a LOW spade at trick one. The play of the ten from partner's point of view is ambiguous —it might be from 10x or K10x. When declarer attacks diamonds, play your highest diamond, once again trying to attract partner's attention to hearts.

(6)
SECOND HAND PLAY

"Second hand low" and "cover an honor with an honor" are somewhat akin to "third hand high" and "always return partner's suit". These little adages may get you by, but won't see you through. Second hand must become familiar with basic positions and must try to foil declarer's plan- frequently by playing second hand high.

BASICS

204. When declarer leads low from dummy, second hand USUALLY plays low and SOMETIMES gives count. Count is important when declarer attacks dummy's long suit and there are no certain side entries to dummy. It is also important when declarer attacks an unbid "mystery" suit.

205* Second hand cannot give attitude by playing a high or a low spot card. These plays will be interpreted as count cards.

North (dummy)
76

East (you)
K10852

Versus suit, if dummy leads low, play the deuce, count. A play of a higher card will also be interpreted as count.

SPLITTING HONORS; PLAY FROM EQUALS

206** When splitting"equal honors"(usually with three or four), SPLIT WITH THE SAME HONOR YOU WOULD HAVE LED; the jack from J109(x) , the queen from QJ10(x).

207** Splitting with the jack shows either J109(x)(x) or KQJ(x). (The exception because you would have led the king). Partner WILL be able to tell the difference. The J109 possibility is more common as declarer is unlikely to be attacking a suit missing the KQJ, particularly at a suit contract.

208* When splitting with TWO equal honors (rare), split with the higher; however split with the king holding either the KQ(x) or the AK(x).

209** When splitting with Q109(x) or K109(x) split with the card you would have led — much easier for partner to read.

210. When dummy's holding has you overwhelmed, play low.

North (dummy)
AK10

West
QJ763

East
982

South
54

If declarer starts this suit early, play low. If declarer starts the suit later in the hand, you may wish to split if you KNOW that declarer cannot get back to her hand to repeat the finesse.

211. The number of tricks needed to defeat the contract is the deciding factor when it comes to splitting honors.

North (dummy)
A105

West (you)
(a) KJ76
(b) KQ76

Assume this is a side suit vs. a suit contract, and declarer leads low. If all you need is ONE trick to defeat the contract, split; otherwise play low.

212* When FOLLOWING SUIT with a three or four card sequence in the trump suit, play highest-lowest.

North
97

West (you)
QJ108

East
6

South
AK5432

When South leads the ace, play the QUEEN. When South continues with the king, play the eight. Now partner knows as much about the trump distribution as the declarer- a primary defensive goal.

213* Versus suit, when dummy has a number of SECONDARY equals, declarer an almost certain singleton and the defenders each have one PRIMARY equal, best defense is for the player BEHIND the equals (you), to win the first trick.

	North (dummy)	
	QJ109	
West		**East** (you)
A765		K432
	South	
	8	

No matter who leads the suit (including you), it is best if the king takes the first lead in the suit.

SECOND HAND HIGH

214. Versus notrump when declarer has TWO stoppers in the suit that has been led and the defenders have two vital entries, the defender with the SHORTER holding in the suit that has been led should turn headstands to use her entry first.

	North (dummy)	
East-West vul. **Dealer South**	♠ Q5 ♥ Q103 ♦ 10964 ♣ J765	
West ♠ 1083 ♥ KJ9765 ♦ A32 ♣ 2		**East** (you) ♠ K9762 ♥ 82 ♦ K5 ♣ 10943
	South ♠ AJ4 ♥ A4 ♦ QJ87 ♣ AKQ8	

South	**West**	**North**	**East**
2NT	Pass	3NT	All Pass

Opening lead: ♥7

Dummy wins the first trick with the ten and a low diamond is advanced. Seize the moment! You have shortness in partner's suit so it is your duty to TRY to use your "in card" first. Play the ♦K and hope partner has the ♦A. If you do, declarer has no chance; if you don't, you have no chance.

Neither side vul.	**North** (dummy)
Dealer North	♠ Q109
	♥ K1063
	♦ J103
	♣ AK4

West		**East** (you)
♠ J32		♠ 7654
♥ 54		♥ A2
♦ K98		♦ A7542
♣ QJ1062		♣ 73

South
♠ AK8
♥ QJ987
♦ Q6
♣ 985

North	**East**	**South**	**West**
1♣	Pass	1♥	Pass
2♥	Pass	4♥	All Pass

Opening lead: ♣Q

Same principle. The first time diamonds are led, you must win the ace and return a club in order to establish a club trick before partner's ♦K is removed. If partner wins the first diamond, the club winner vanishes. (No club to lead upon winning the ♦A).

215* When you are the danger hand, play second hand high to prevent declarer from ducking the lead into partner's hand. Declarers hate defenders who do this.

East-West vul.
Dealer South

North (dummy)
♠ AK1095
♥ Q94
♦ 73
♣ 876

West (you)
♠ Q64
♥ J6
♦ Q10965
♣ QJ4

East
♠ J87
♥ K108732
♦ 8
♣ 932

South
♠ 32
♥ A5
♦ AKJ42
♣ AK105

South	West	North	East
1♦	Pass	1♠	Pass
3♣	Pass	3♠	Pass
3NT	All Pass		

Opening lead: ♥J

The play to trick one goes jack, queen, king, ace. On the assumption that partner has good hearts, you are the danger hand. When a spade is led, play the queen. If dummy ducks, a heart is ruinous; if dummy wins, the spades are dead.

216. Versus suit or notrump when dummy tables with AJ10(x)(x) and no side entry, second hand high with honor doubleton or honor third can have a paralyzing effect, particularly when declarer has a small doubleton.

North (dummy)
AJ1076

West (you)
K98

East
Q54

South
32

Play the king and kill the suit.. If dummy wins, declarer can be held to one trick; if king is ducked and a later finesse is taken, declarer winds up with zilch.

217* When dummy has AK109(x) and no side entry, play second hand high with Jx or Qx.

(a)

North (dummy)
AK109(x)

West (you)
J2, Q2

East
Q876(x), J876(x)

South
43

When South leads low, play your honor. If South has a doubleton, you save at least one trick, possibly many more.

(b)

North (dummy)
AK98

West (you)
(1) QJx
(2) Q10x
(3) J10x

East
(1) 10xxx
(2) Jxxx
(3) Qxxx

South
xx

Notrump, dummy has no side entry and declarer is known to have a doubleton. When declarer leads low, insert an honor to save a trick. If you play low, declarer can play the nine and take an eventual three tricks. If you play an honor, declarer gets only two. Play the same if dummy has AQ97 (declarer may have 8x).

218. Play second hand high with AQx if declarer lacks an entry to lead the suit through you a second time.

Both sides vul.
Dealer **South**

North (dummy)
♠ 876
♥ AQJ76
♦ J109
♣ 32

West
♠ -
♥ 1043
♦ 7632
♣ J109865

East (you)
♠ AQ3
♥ K985
♦ Q854
♣ 74

South
♠ KJ109542
♥ 2
♦ AK
♣ AKQ

South	West	North	East
2♣	Pass	2♥	Pass
2♠	Pass	3♠	Pass
4NT	Pass	5♦	Pass
6 ♠	All Pass		

Opening lead: ♣J

Declarer wins, crosses to dummy with a heart and plays a spade. Win the ace; declarer has no way to return to dummy to repeat the spade finesse.

South
♠ KJ109542
♥ 2
♦ AK
♣ AKQ

South	**West**	**North**	**East**
2♣	Pass	2♥	Pass
2♠	Pass	3♠	Pass
4NT	Pass	5♦	Pass
6 ♠	All Pass		

Opening lead: ♣J

Declarer wins, crosses to dummy with a heart and plays a spade. Win the ace; declarer has no way to return to dummy to repeat the spade finesse.

219* If dummy wins the opening lead with a singleton honor; declarer is marked with at least the ace. Versus suit, be wary of letting declarer get back to her hand to discard a loser from dummy on that ace.

Both sides vul.
Dealer **South**

North (dummy)
♠ K
♥ 9742
♦ 62
♣ KJ10752

West
♠ QJ1032
♥ 10
♦ AQ109
♣ 984

East (you)
♠ 976
♥ A3
♦ 87543
♣ A63

South
♠ A854
♥ KQJ865
♦ KJ
♣ Q

South	**West**	**North**	**East**
1♥	1♠	4♥	All Pass

Opening lead: ♠Q

If declarer tries to sneak back to her hand with either a trump or a club, rise and shine. Win either ace and return a diamond before declarer can discard a diamond on the ♠A.

220* Play second hand high with the ace when the trick count tells you that declarer is trying to steal the contract fulfilling trick from a great player like you.

North-South vul.
Dealer South

North (dummy)
♠ AQ3
♥ 32
♦ AKQ109
♣ 875

West
♠ J1086
♥ A1054
♦ J3
♣ J62

East (you)
♠ 975
♥ QJ97
♦ 842
♣ A94

South
♠ K42
♥ K86
♦ 765
♣ KQ103

South	**West**	**North**	**East**
Pass	Pass	1♦	Pass
2NT	Pass	3NT	All Pass

Opening lead: ♠J (Jack denies)

Declarer wins in dummy and leads a club at trick two. Are you awake? Declarer appears to have three spade tricks to go along with five diamond tricks. Do not let declarer steal the contract. Go up with the ♣A and return the ♥Q hoping partner has ♥A10xx. Are you a great player, or what?

Neither side vul.
Dealer South

North (dummy)
♠ J76
♥ K109
♦ KQ75
♣ J103

West
♠ Q10842
♥ J43
♦ 86
♣ Q42

East (you)
♠ A93
♥ 8652
♦ 1032
♣ A76

South
♠ K5
♥ AQ7
♦ AJ95
♣ K985

South	**West**	**North**	**East**
1NT	Pass	3NT	All Pass

Opening lead: ♠ 4

You play the ace and nine of spades at tricks one and two, noticing partner's second play of the deuce confirming a five card suit. The first time a club is played, rise, and take the setting tricks in the spade suit.

221* If you can determine that declarer is attempting to create an extra dummy entry by taking a finesse, second hand high (or ducking an honor) can kill the extra entry.

North (dummy)
AJ6

West (you)
K943

East
10872

South
Q5

If you KNOW that declarer needs TWO dummy entries, duck the queen, but play the king if declarer leads the five.

222. Every book should have at least one insulting tip. Ready? Do not force high cards out of the dummy for no particular reason.

North (dummy)
K84

West (you)
J963

East
Q

South
A10752

When declarer leads low towards the king, don't even think about playing the nine to drive out the king. Declarer was going to play the king anyway. Playing the nine is a sub prekindergarten play or worse!

INFERENCES

223* Before taking a trick when declarer leads low towards honor strength in the dummy, ask yourself if declarer can have the holding you fear. If the answer is no, it might be wiser to play low.

(a)

North (dummy)
J10643

West (you)
Q92

East
K8

South
A75

Versus notrump, declarer leads low towards dummy. Should you play the queen? Clearly it is right to play the queen if declarer has AKx. However with AKx, declarer would start with the king and ace. As partner is marked with at least one high honor, play low.

(b)

North (dummy)
Q1084

West (you)
K95

East
J2

South
A763

Versus suit or notrump, declarer cashes the ace and then leads low. Play the nine (in tempo!) as partner is marked with the jack. If declarer had both the ace and the jack, the suit would have been started by leading an honor from dummy.

(c)

	North (dummy) KJ94	
West (you) A75		**East** Q108
	South 632	

When declarer leads up to a KJ9 combination, not only is it right to duck the first time in case partner has the queen, it may be right to duck the second time as well, in case partner has the ten.

(d)

	North (dummy) KQ107	
West (you) A854		**East** J6
	South 932	

When declarer leads up to a KQ10 combination, duck twice, giving declarer a chance to finesse the ten.

(e)

	North (dummy) AJ92	
West (you) KQ76		**East** 1084
	South 53	

When you see a AJ9(x) combination to your left, play low with the KQx(x). If declarer has two or three small cards, the percentage play for two tricks is the nine — just what you want.

(f)

Alternatively when you see AJ9(x) to your left and you have Q10x or K10x, play the honor if you think partner has the other honor. Declarer may think you have KQx(x), win the ace, reenter her hand and lead low to the jack.

(g)

	North (dummy) Q1085	
West (you) AK73		**East** J94
	South 62	

When you see Q10x(x) to your left and you hold AKx(x), play low when declarer leads up to the dummy. Declarer's normal play is the ten.

(h) **North** (dummy)
K1095

West (you)
A73

East
QJ6

South
842

When declarer leads up to a K109(x) combination in dummy, duck TWICE. The percentage play for declarer is low to the ten and then low to the nine. Perfect.

(i) **North** (dummy)
QJ109

West (you)
K652

East
?

South
?

Versus notrump (or suit), it is almost always right to play low. If declarer had the ace, the suit would have been initiated from dummy. In addition, vs. suit, if declarer has a singleton, it is far better to allow partner to win the first trick. (See tip 213).

224. At a suit contract, when declarer leads from a small doubleton in dummy and inserts the ten (or lower) and partner wins the trick, play partner for the king as well.

North (dummy)
64

West
KJ(x)

East (you)
A932

South
Q1087(x)

Declarer's first play is low from dummy to the ten and jack. When the suit is led a second time, play low. Partner has the king and it could be blank. Even if partner has KJx, it is better to allow partner to win the second trick.

225. All rules about second hand low go out the window when winning the trick will defeat the contract while playing low might allow declarer to make the hand.

GIVING COUNT

226. The weaker your hand, the more likely you are to give honest count signals. Most important is to give honest count with worthless cards when dummy's long suit is attacked – particularly when there are no side entries to dummy.

North (dummy)
AQJ105

West (you)
(1) 84
(2) 842
(3) 8642
(4) K83
(5) K832

When declarer leads up to this holding, give honest count with (1), (2) and (3); with (4) or (5), it is optional.

227** Vs. notrump when dummy's suit is solid or semi-solid and there IS a side entry to dummy, give suit preference rather than count.

North (dummy)
KQJ108

West (you)
9752

East
A6

South
43

When declarer leads low towards this combination partner will probably be more interested in knowing what to play after winning the ace than in knowing your count.

228* When declarer leads a side suit from dummy in which declarer's length is known, do NOT give count. If declarer's length is unknown, tend to give count.

229. When holding ALL of the partnership strength, there is no need to give honest count signals. What do these signals matter to a partner who won't be on lead until the next hand?

230. Avoid giving count vs. slams with the strong hand; the weaker hand gives honest count far more often.

231 If partner doesn't watch your cards and declarer does, avoid giving count; if partner watches every card you play like a hawk and declarer could care less, give count.

WHEN AN HONOR IS LED FROM THE CLOSED HAND

232. There are two overriding considerations when deciding whether to cover an honor: (1) CAN I PROMOTE ANYTHING FOR MYSELF OR MY PARTNER? (2) PARTNER'S LENGTH. Often the answer to (1) depends upon (2).

233. If promotion is impossible or unlikely, do NOT cover.

WHEN AN HONOR IS LED FROM THE CLOSED HAND—THE QUEEN

234. When declarer leads the queen from KNOWN length towards Axx in dummy, assume declarer has the jack and quite likely the ten.

North (dummy)
A52

West (you)	**East**
(1) K6	(1) 9843
(2) K63	(2) 985
(3) K643	(3) 98

South
QJ107

Assume declarer is known to have four cards in this suit and leads the queen: With (1) Cover. Partner has four cards and one may be promotable. With (2) play low. Declarer may have QJ9x. If you cover, you put partner's ten at risk. With (3) play low and guarantee yourself a fourth round trick.

235. When the stronger honors are visible to your left and an honor is led from the closed hand, if you can promote nothing for yourself, partner's length is critical.

(a)

North (dummy)
AJ104

West (you)
K52

East
?

South
Q

Cover the queen if partner is marked with four cards. If partner has fewer, do not cover.

(b)

North (dummy)
AJ4

West (you)
K763

East
?

South
Q

If partner is marked with a singleton or doubleton, do not cover. If partner can have three (or more) cards, cover; partner may have 10xx(x).

WHEN AN HONOR IS LED FROM THE CLOSED HAND—THE JACK

236* When declarer leads the jack from the closed hand towards the ace, and partner has an equal honor, do not cover if declarer has no hand reentry to repeat the finesse; if declarer has a reentry, cover if promotion is possible.

North (dummy)
(1) A1098
(2) A1084

West (you)
K53

East
?

South
J

With (1), do not cover, no promotion is possible. With (2), if declarer has a hand reentry, cover. Partner may have Q9x(x). If declarer has no hand reentry, play low and allow partner to take her queen; you will make your king later. To cover would be disastrous if declarer had J9x.

237. When you know from the bidding that partner cannot have any missing ace or king, do not use a queen to cover a lower honor unless you can promote a nine or ten in partner's hand.

North (dummy)
A1094

West (you)
Q5

East
?

South
J

If South is marked with the king, do not cover. However, if partner can have K8xx(x) cover. If this is the trump suit, do not even think of covering. Declarer may have KJ8x or KJ8xx and may be planning to finesse into you, not through you!

238* If the bidding has marked either you or partner with a specific honor, there is more reason to cover in an otherwise doubtful position.

North (dummy)
K6

West (you)
Q9543

East
A1072

South
J8

If partner is absolutely marked with the ace, cover the jack as declarer may be trying an "Indonesian" finesse (a finesse that cannot possibly work if you cover).

239* When declarer must decide which of two finesses to take to land the contract, and you can see that one works while the other doesn't, cover nothing.

IMPs
Both sides vul.
Dealer **North**

North (dummy)
♠ AQ7
♥ 54
♦ AQJ105
♣ AQ4

West (you)
♠ K1096
♥ KJ932
♦ 43
♣ 85

East
♠ 832
♥ Q876
♦ 96
♣ KJ93

South
♠ J54
♥ A10
♦ K872
♣ 10762

North	**East**	**South**	**West**
1♦	Pass	1NT	Pass
3NT	All Pass		

Opening lead: ♥3

Partner's queen drives out declarer's ace and declarer produces the ♠J at trick two. Duck in tempo. The play of a spade before a diamond indicates that declarer has the ♦K giving North-South eight tricks. Declarer needs an extra trick from one of the black suits. Make no friendly covers. Declarer is desperately looking for a cover. If you duck calmly, declarer may decide to play the ace and take the club finesse instead.

COVERING NINES OR TENS

240. When declarer leads a nine or a ten towards a doubleton or tripleton honor, duck.

(a)
North
Q42
West (you) 1063
East AJ
South
K9875

(b)
North
A75
West (you) J32
East KQ
South
109864

Covering the nine in (a) or the ten in (b) has kindergarten overtones.

241. Before deciding whether or not to cover, visualize what dummy will look like if you cover and what it will look like if you don't.

North (dummy)
AQ93

West (you)
J65

East
K872

South
104

Covering the ten, leaving dummy with A9x,will get you two tricks if partner has K8xx. Ducking and leaving dummy with AQ9, nets you only one as your jack is due to drop.

COVERING HONORS IN THE TRUMP SUIT

242* Covering honors in the trump suit (or any suit) in which partner is marked with shortness (and you have nothing to promote for yourself), has all the earmarks of a death wish.

North (dummy)
A65

West (you)
Q4

East
?

South
J

If South is known to have five or more cards in this suit, covering is out of the question. If declarer has exactly four cards, cover with Q9 doubleton but not with Qx.

243* When there is a singleton trump honor in dummy (jack or queen), covering or not covering depends upon how many trump tricks you need.

(a)

North (dummy)
J

West
(1) 1065
(2) K65

East (you)
Q84

South
(1) AK9732
(2) A109732

If ONE trick is needed, cover; partner needs 10xx or 9xxx. If TWO tricks are needed, duck; partner needs the ace or king.

(b)

North (dummy)
Q

West
(1) 752
(2) J93

East (you)
K84

South
(1) AJ10963
(2) A108765

If you need one trick, duck, because you have it. If you need TWO tricks, cover, hoping partner has J9x or 107xx.

244. Do not cover an honor when you know that declarer isn't about to finesse because of the combined length between declarer and dummy.

North (dummy)
1086

West

East (you)
QJ92

South
AK7543

If declarer has shown a six card suit, do not cover the ten. Declarer is not going to run the ten. For all declarer knows, the suit is dividing 2-2. Declarer is testing your nerves.

245. When partner is marked with the king (or ace) of trump, do not cover a jack or a ten with Qx if you can ruff something and your ruff will be the setting trick.

North-South vul.
Dealer North

North (dummy)
♠ AK1096
♥ J7
♦ Q5
♣ KQ76

West
♠ Q7
♥ K65
♦ J643
♣ J432

East (you)
♠ J832
♥ Q3
♦ AK982
♣ A5

South
♠ 54
♥ A109842
♦ 107
♣ 1098

North	East	South	West
1♠	2♦	Pass	3♦
Pass	Pass	3♥	All Pass

Opening lead: ♦3

You cash two diamonds and exit with ace and a club to dummy's queen. At trick five the ♥J is led from dummy. Don't cover. Declarer cannot have both the ace and king of hearts and bid this way. As partner is marked with a heart honor, play low and ruff the club return. If you cover, your lose your ruff.

WHEN AN HONOR IS LED FROM DUMMY

246. When there are two or more equal honors in dummy, cover the last equal- but even then only when promotion is possible.

North (dummy)
J108

West
Q

East (you)
K72

South
A96543

Resounding "crashes" like this can happen when you cover the first equal; nor will partner be terribly thrilled if you cover the second. However, if partner has Q9x, you save a trick by covering the second honor. Once again, partner's length is critical.

247* When there are two equal honors in dummy, you have a doubleton honor and you suspect partner has FOUR card length, cover the FIRST equal; otherwise, play low.

North (dummy)
J104

West
9732

East (you)
Q8

South
AK63

Covering the jack limits declarer to three tricks, playing low gives her four.

248. By covering the second of equals, you may prevent declarer from taking a marked finesse against one of your own lower intermediates.

North (dummy)
J104

West
5

East (you)
K973

South
AQ862

If you cover the jack, declarer wins, returns to dummy with the ten and takes the proven finesse against your remaining 97. If you duck the jack and cover the ten, declarer knows you have the guarded nine, but with no return entry to dummy, can do nothing about it.

249. When dummy has KQx and declarer has known length, duck the first honor holding A10xx.

North (dummy)
KQ5

West
3

East (you)
A1086

South
J9742

If you win the first honor, you are susceptible to a later finesse against your ten. If you win the second honor, declarer needs a return entry to dummy to repeat the finesse. The ducking play also works well when declarer has J9xx.

250. At notrump ducking twice when dummy has KQ blank is usually a winning play to prevent long suit establishment.

	North (dummy)	
	KQ	
West		**East**
852		A96
	South	
	J10743	

Duck twice and declarer will need TWO hand entries to establish and cash the suit; duck twice and find partner with Jxx and you will need TWO bodyguards.

251. Covering the second of equals may protect partner from a return finesse.

	North (dummy)	
	QJ6	
West		**East** (you)
1032		K54
	South	
	A987	

If you cover the jack (or queen), partner's ten is vulnerable to a return finesse. If you duck the first honor and cover the second, partner's ten lives!

252* When dummy has J10 or QJ doubleton, covering the first honor may block the suit and is the stronger play.

(a)	**North** (dummy)	
	J10	
West		**East** (you)
932		Q74
	South	
	AK865	

Cover the first honor. The cover works particularly well if declarer has no other hand entries.

(b)	**North** (dummy)	
	QJ	
West		**East** (you)
1032		K54
	South	
	A9876	

Cover the first honor and make life miserable for the declarer. If the position is reversed and declarer has the two honors doubleton, second hand, if she can diagnose the position, should also cover the first honor.

253. When you have a doubleton honor and partner has at most a doubleton, cover only against close family.

North (dummy)
J43

West
K

East
Q7

South
A1098652

Do not cover the jack if South has advertised a six card suit or longer unless you are into "crashes".

254 When declarer sets about establishing a suit in which dummy has a singleton queen or king, it is usually right to duck the first round with the ace. It complicates communications for the declarer.

North (dummy)
K

West
943

East
A862

South
QJ1075

In notrump, declarer would be very pleased if you took the king.

255. There is no point in covering a singleton honor led from dummy if you know declarer has no side entries to her hand.

North (dummy)
J

West
843

East (you)
Q65

South
AK10972

Duck the jack if **South** has no hand reentry.

256* Possession of strong intermediate spot cards is the tip off to covering an honor.

North (dummy)
J2

West
?

East (you)
(1) K9863
(2) K6543

South
?

If declarer is likely to have three cards, cover; if declarer is likely to have a four card suit, cover with (1); play low with (2) because declarer's spot cards are surely stronger than yours.

MISCELLANEOUS

257* When you know that declarer has her contract in the bag and taking a finesse would risk that contract, cover nothing. Declarer is not about to risk her contract for an overtrick unless (1) you are marked with the honor; (2) you are playing tournament bridge; (3) You are sitting too close to the table.

North (dummy)
AJ54

West (you)
K1098

East
632

South
Q7

Under "normal" conditions, cover the queen to promote your secondary intermediates. However, if declarer cannot afford to take the finesse, duck.

258. Be nonchalant when not covering; even if it is wrong, declarer may think you don't have the missing honor.

259. In order to be nonchalant when not covering, you must be prepared. Hesitating and then not covering is a dead giveaway.

260. No matter how much you know about covering or not covering you are still at risk against a weak declarer. An impossible cover against a strong declarer may become a mandatory cover against a weaker one.

North (dummy)
A7

West
K32

East
?

South
Q

Against a strong declarer, covering in this position is wrong. Against a weak player who might not have the jack you will look like a fool if you don't cover. You must learn to live with the right plays even if they turn out badly.

261* When declarer leads a known singleton towards a KQx(x) combination in dummy, playing low usually saves a trick even though you lose your ace.

Neither side vul.
Dealer North

North (dummy)
♠ KQ96
♥ 982
♦ A32
♣ K64

West (you)
♠ AJ52
♥ QJ105
♦ 74
♣ J98

East
♠ 10843
♥ 743
♦ 86
♣ Q1052

South
♠ 5
♥ AK6
♦ KQJ1098
♣ A73

North	**East**	**South**	**West**
1NT*	Pass	4♣**	Pass
4♥***	Pass	6♦ All Pass	

* 12-14
** Gerber
*** One ace

Opening lead: ♥Q

Declarer wins the opening lead, partner discouraging, and leads a low spade. If you rise, declarer eventually discards a heart and a club on the established spades. If you play low, you lose your ace, but you get a heart and a club in return.

262* At a suit contract if dummy leads a singleton towards known length and you have the ace with length and there are not enough trump in dummy to ruff out your ace, play low. The trick usually comes back with interest.

Both sides vul.
Dealer North

North (dummy)
♠ J10
♥ AJ1076
♦ 4
♣ QJ765

West
♠ 62
♥ K832
♦ Q7
♣ K1084

East (you)
♠ 843
♥ Q94
♦ A8432
♣ 932

South
♠ AKQ975
♥ 5
♦ KJ1096
♣ A

North	**East**	**South**	**West**
Pass	Pass	1♠	Pass
2♥	Pass	3♦	Pass
3♠	Pass	4NT	Pass
5♦	Pass	6♠	All Pass

Opening lead: ♣4

At trick two declarer crosses to a heart and leads a diamond. Do not even think about going up with your ace. Even if declarer has the ♦K and plays it, declarer cannot ruff out your ace and you break out even. Your big reward comes when declarer has a KJ10 combination and plays the jack or partner has the king.

263* When length protects your key honor(s), do not cover.

North (dummy)
94

West
?

East (you)
K32, K532

South
?

If partner is known to have four cards in the suit cover the nine with Kxx, but play low with Kxxx.

264* When you know that declarer is planning a likely double finesse against you and it is going to work, do not cover the first honor.

North (dummy)
J73

West
2

East (you)
K1064

South
AQ985

If South is marked with a five card suit, do not cover the jack. If you do, South will win and probably reenter dummy to run the seven. If you don't cover, South is apt to play low to the queen and you will wind up with a trick.

(7)
DISCARDING

Discarding properly is an important element of good defense. Attitude discards should be clear, but even more important is knowing which suit(s) to discard and which suits to save!

METHODS

265. If you can handle switching from one method to another, upside down discards (low encourages-high discourages) are more efficient because they are less wasteful.

	North (dummy)	
	102	
West		**East** (you)
94		AQJ83
	South	
	K765	

If you discard the ♥8, declarer suddenly has two stoppers. Best is to make a discouraging discard(s) in another suit (see tip #275). However, if you must discard from this suit, it make more sense to discard the three to show strength.

Another popular discarding convention is "Lavinthal". In the simplest version, the discard of an odd spot card (3-5-7-9) is encouraging in that suit. The discard of an even spot card (2,4,6,8) is discouraging and carries suit preference overtones. A low-even spot card discard asks for the lower ranking suit, a high-even discard asks for the higher ranking suit.

A. LENGTH PARITY DISCARDS

266* When discarding try to keep four card length parity with both declarer and dummy. When in a bind, discard from the suit in which partner has equal or greater length than you.

Neither side vul.
Dealer South

North (dummy)
♠ K76
♥ K432
♦ J5
♣ A876

West
♠ J8
♥ J5
♦ K9832
♣ K1042

East (you)
♠ 10942
♥ 10976
♦ Q10
♣ Q53

South
♠ AQ53
♥ AQ8
♦ A764
♣ J9

South	West	North	East
1NT	Pass	2♣	Pass
2♠	Pass	3NT	All Pass

Opening lead: ♦3

Declarer wins the third diamond, discarding a spade from dummy. What should you discard? This is not an easy problem. Declarer is known to hold four spades (and four diamonds) making a spade discard dangerous. But dummy has both four hearts and four clubs and a rule must be broken. Time to count. Declarer has at MOST three clubs giving partner at least three clubs. Hearts is another story. If declarer has three hearts, partner only has two. Hearts is the suit to save. DISCARD FROM THE SUIT IN WHICH PARTNER HAS EQUAL OR GREATER LENGTH THAN YOU. Discard a club.

267* If partner needs a primary honor in dummy's four card suit, to defeat the contract, assume she has it and don't worry about length parity.

North (dummy)
Q1087

West (you)
J943

East

South

If partner needs either the ace or king to defeat the contract, it is safe to discard from this suit. At worst, you will be giving up an overtrick.

268* If partner needs a SECONDARY honor in dummy's four card card suit to defeat the contract, assume she has it, and don't worry about keeping length parity.

North (dummy)
AK107

East (you)
J943

If partner needs the queen to defeat the contract, assume she has it. If so, you can afford to make one discard in this suit and still retain a winner.

269. When a suit is blocked and there is NO dummy entry, it may not be necessary to keep length parity.

North (dummy)
K1087

West
652

East (you)
J943

South
AQ

If South is marked with a doubleton and there is no side entry to dummy, it is safe to discard once from this suit. If South unblocks the suit, it is safe to discard twice.

270* When you and partner each have four cards in dummy's strong four card suit, it is usually safe for one of you (but not both) to discard from that suit.

North (dummy)
AKQ2

West
J875

East (you)
10963

South
4

If the bidding marks declarer with a singleton, you can afford to discard from this suit as long as partner's doesn't (and vice-versa).

271* If declarer is KNOWN to have a STRONG four card suit, and you have a weakish four card holding, be careful about discarding from this suit.

North (dummy)
93

West (you)
8642

East
J105

South
AKQ7

A discard from you in this suit is instant disaster.

272. If dummy has a four or five card suit and you have four cards in the suit and your highest card is higher than dummy's fourth highest card, do not discard from this suit.

(a)

North (dummy)
AKQ9

West
J5

East (you)
10762

South
843

It is life threatening to discard from this suit; your highest card is higher than dummy's fourth highest card.

(b)

North (dummy)
AKQ63

West
J9

East (you)
7542

South
108

Don't even think of discarding from this suit. That little seven of yours is higher than dummy's fourth highest card, the six.

DISCARDING FROM LENGTH

273. Versus suit contracts tend to make discards from length, particularly KNOWN length; discarding from shortness frequently exposes partner's honor holding in the suit.

(a)

	North (dummy)	
	K1032	
West (you)		**East**
84		Q76
	South	
	AJ95	

An early discard here gives away the location of partner's queen.

(b)

	North (dummy)	
	AK5	
West (you)		**East**
83		J972
	South	
	Q1064	

A discard in this suit exposes partner to a marked finesse when you show out on the second round.

(c)

	North (dummy)	
	KQ5	
West		**East** (you)
J93		742
	South	
	A1086	

If declarer is marked with the ace, a discard from either you or partner, gives away the show. (If declarer thinks you have four cards in this suit, she'll play king, queen and low to the ten.)

274* Holding a small doubleton and seeing AKx in dummy, hang on to your doubleton. When holding xxx or xxxx and seeing the AKQ10 in dummy, once again hang on. In both cases a discard may expose partner's jack.

	North (dummy)	
	AKQ10	
West (you)		**East**
8643		J75
	South	
	92	

If declarer needs four tricks from this combination , the percentage play is to finesse the ten. However, if you discard wantonly from this suit, declarer will surely forego the finesse.

NEGATIVE DISCARDS (SAVING THE GOOD STUFF)

275. Versus notrump tend to make negative discards in suits you don't want led as opposed to positive discards in suits you do want led. Given an opportunity to make two discards, make a negative discard in each of the suits you have no interest in, saving all of your goodies in the suit you cherish.

North South vul.
Dealer South

	North (dummy)	
	♠ J1054	
	♥ Q109	
	♦ A76	
	♣ K65	
West		**East** (you)
♠ K9863		♠ -
♥ 753		♥ AKJ8
♦ J10		♦ 95432
♣ J104		♣ 8732
	South	
	♠ AQ72	
	♥ 642	
	♦ KQ8	
	♣ AQ9	

South	**West**	**North**	**East**
1NT	Pass	3NT	All Pass

Opening lead: ♠6

Discard a discouraging diamond on the first spade and a discouraging club on the second (or vice versa). A heart discard puts you in the back of the nursery school class (last row).

276* When able to make only ONE discard and not wanting to make a discard in the suit you want led, make a negative discard in the suit partner is more likely to want to lead. No sense wasting a negative discard in a suit partner has no intention of leading.

Both sides vul.
Dealer South

North (dummy)
♠ 8763
♥ 32
♦ 962
♣ J1098

East (you)
♠ KQJ92
♥ 8
♦ AJ73
♣ 653

South	**West**	**North**	**East**
2♣	Pass	2♦	Pass
2NT	All Pass		

Opening lead: ♥6

Declarer wins the ♥9 and returns the ♥K to partner's ace. What do you discard?

You want a spade shift badly but you don't want to waste a spade to get it. As partner is unlikely to shift to a club, make a discouraging discard in DIAMONDS. If partner switches to a spade, the hand is defeated.

Declarer's hand: ♠ A54 ♥ KQJ9 ♦ KQ10 ♣ AKQ
Partner's hand: ♠ 10 ♥ A107654 ♦ 854 ♣ 742

Neither side vul.
Dealer East

North (dummy)
♠ 1093
♥ 763
♦ AQJ10
♣ 654

West (you)
♠ J52
♥ 94
♦ 8632
♣ 9732

East	**South**	**West**	**North**
1♥	Dbl.	Pass	2♦
Pass	2♠	Pass	3♠
Pass	4♠	All Pass	

Opening lead: ♥9

Partner wins the first three heart tricks. What do you discard on the third heart?

First, ask yourself what you want partner to lead. The answer is a fourth heart in order to promote your ♠J. Next ask yourself how you can coax partner to lead that suit. Since partner is not about to shift to a diamond, discard a discouraging club.

Declarer's hand: ♠ AKQ86 ♥ 1085 ♦ K5 ♣ AK8
Partner's hand: ♠ 74 ♥ AKQJ2 ♦ 974 ♣ QJ10

HONOR DISCARDS (NOT SHOWING OFF—SHOWING STRENGTH)

277. The discard of an honor shows the TOP of a sequence of honors. The discard of a king shows KQJ10(x), the discard of the queen shows QJ109(x), etc. The discard of an ace if it isn't an unblock of some sort, is a very sad discard, it tells partner you started with the AKQ etc. and she has led the wrong suit –again.

Both sides vul.
Dealer South

North (dummy).
♠ Q7
♥ K53
♦ 8762
♣ KQJ8

West
♠ 10542
♥ 10987
♦ K3
♣ 763

East (you)
♠ J63
♥ 62
♦ QJ1095
♣ 1054

South
♠ AK98
♥ AQJ4
♦ A4
♣ A92

South plays 7NT and West leads the ♥10. Assume declarer begins by rattling off four rounds of hearts. On the third heart, discard the ♦Q. This tells partner two things: (1) you have a strong sequence in diamonds headed by the queen; (2) partner can discard diamonds. Now on the fourth club partner can discard a diamond, blanking the king, rather than a spade; a discard which allows declarer to make the grand slam!

278* The discard of an honor in a previously led suit tells partner that it is your highest remaining equal.

North (dummy)
63

West (you)
Q98742

East
105

South
AKJ

Your lead of the seven goes to the ten and the jack. Later, if you discard the queen, partner will know declarer remains with the ace and king. If you have not had a chance to make a discard, and partner returns the suit, play the queen for the same reason.

COUNT DISCARDS

279** When discarding from a suit partner has led, discard the same card you would have returned, present count.

North (dummy)
86

West
4

East (you)
(1) K73 (7)
(2) K732 (2)
(3) KJ752 (7)
(4) KJ7532 (2)

You play the king and it loses. Later, if you wish to discard from this suit, make a present count discard, the same card you would have returned.

280** When discarding TWICE from the same suit, the FIRST discard is ATTITUDE, the SECOND, PRESENT COUNT.

(1) 942 (2) (9)
(2) 9432 (2) (3)
(3) KQ987 (9) (8)
(4) KQ9872 (9) (2)

This table assumes "standard" attitude discards. If you play upside down, the second card is still present count.

281* When declarer (with no dummy entry) has all the tricks but one and starts peeling off winners (usually a long trump suit), and you have a worthless hand, give partner count by voiding yourself in your shortest suit at once. Don't make random discards.

282* Versus suit, a discard in dummy's solid suit is count; vs notrump, suit preference.

Both sides vul.
Dealer West

North (dummy)
♠ 2
♥ 762
♦ 97
♣ AKQJ763

West
♠ -
♥ J5
♦ AKQJ10654
♣ 1094

East (you)
♠ 98653
♥ Q10943
♦ 2
♣ 82

South
♠ AKQJ1074
♥ AK8
♦ 83
♣ 5

West	North	East	South
5♦	Pass	Pass	5♠
All Pass			

Opening lead: ♦A

When partner cashes a second diamond, discard the ♣ 8, count. Now it is safe for partner to lead a club and kill dummy. If declarer plays a second club, you will ruff and eventually come to a heart trick.

NEWSPAPER COLUMN DISCARDS—LOOKING FOR GLORY

283. If you can tell from the rule of 11 that partner's suit is ready to run, (but partner can't) an honor discard in the suit is the answer.

North (dummy)
76

West
A10853

East (you)
QJ9

South
K42

Partner leads the five and the jack loses to the king. Since you can tell from the "rule" that declarer has no other card higher than the five, you can afford to discard the queen to give partner the good news. Remember, partner doesn't know who has the queen when you play the jack.

284* Assume you can discard a loser on one of partner's winners; if you can arrange to reduce to a singleton in another suit first, you can discard that singleton and then get a ruff. Would you like this tip repeated in English, or perhaps an example (yes, please) would be better.

Both sides vul.
Dealer West

North (dummy)
♠ Q106
♥ QJ53
♦ J106
♣ K86

West (you)
♠ 742
♥ AK10
♦ A2
♣ J9732

East
♠ 83
♥ 942
♦ KQ984
♣ Q54

South
♠ AKJ95
♥ 876
♦ 753
♣ A10

West	**North**	**East**	**South**
1♣	Pass	1♦	1♠
Pass	2♠	All Pass	

Opening lead: ♥A

Partner plays a low heart and you try the ♦A which is greeted by an enthusiastic signal. Before rushing to play a second diamond, cash the ♥K first. If partner has both missing diamond honors, you will be able to discard the ♥10 and ruff the heart return to defeat the contract one trick.

285. If a spectacular discard is what it may take to defeat a contract, go for it!

Both sides vul.
Dealer North

North (dummy)
♠ K108642
♥ J
♦ J83
♣ AQ4

West (you)
♠ AJ
♥ 10732
♦ 2
♣ 1097532

East
♠ Q9753
♥ 8
♦ AKQ1075
♣ J

South
♠ -
♥ AKQ9654
♦ 964
♣ K86

North	East	South	West
1♠	2♦	2♥	Pass
2♠	Pass	4♥	All Pass

Opening lead: ♦2

When partner wins the first diamond with the ten and continues with the ace, there is a great chance you will be able to make two discards. Why tempt fate? Discard both spades. When partner returns a spade, your ♥10 will be promoted.

286* When partner has an established suit with no certain outside entry, consider an unblock in the suit declarer must establish.

Neither side vul.
Dealer East

North (dummy)
♠ Q
♥ K72
♦ AJ109853
♣ Q4

West (you)
♠ J
♥ 10854
♦ K4
♣ 1097653

East
♠ A109872
♥ QJ3
♦ Q6
♣ 82

South
♠ K6543
♥ A96
♦ 72
♣ AKJ

East	**South**	**West**	**North**
2♠	2NT	Pass	3NT
All Pass			

Opening lead: ♠J

Partner wins the ace and returns the ten of spades to declarer's king. Want to see your name in lights? Discard the ♦K! If declarer has the queen, your king is worthless; if partner has the queen, you are famous!

ALARM CARD DISCARDS

287. Don't forget the "alarm card discard" especially designed for partners who tend to fall asleep. An alarm card discard is the discard of an unusually high card in an uncalled for situation to wake partner up. It warns partner NOT to make a normal looking play.

East-West vul.
Dealer East

North (dummy)
♠ KQJ2
♥ 76
♦ J5
♣ KJ1094

West (you)
♠ A109876
♥ 2
♦ Q4
♣ 8752

East
♠ 543
♥ AKJ1098
♦ 32
♣ 63

South
♠ -
♥ Q543
♦ AK109876
♣ AQ

East	South	West	North
2♥	4♦	Pass	5♦
All Pass			

Opening lead: ♥2

On the second heart discard the ♠A! This little brilliancy sends partner two messages: (1) don't lead spades! (2) lead hearts as you cannot possibly have the ♣A. Why can't you have the ♣A? (1) How could you have two aces plus a singleton in partner's suit and not double 5♦? (2) If you had the ♣A, why not ruff the second round of hearts and cash it? Bridge is an easy game. If you have the contract defeated, defeat it.

North (dummy)
KJ65

West
A83

East (you)
Q10942

South
7

If you know declarer has a singleton and you want partner to grab the ace the first time the suit is led, discard the queen.

288* Discarding a TRUMP (trumping partner's ace) in order to cash the setting trick is one way to avoid anxiety and stress. (See previous tip)

North-South vul.
Dealer West

North (dummy)
♠ 93
♥ J63
♦ KQ98
♣ QJ107

West (you)
♠ 862
♥ 92
♦ A32
♣ 87432

East
♠ 76
♥ AKQ108
♦ 107654
♣ 9

South
♠ AKQJ105
♥ 754
♦ J
♣ AK5

West	**North**	**East**	**South**
Pass	Pass	2♥	4♠

All Pass

Opening lead: ♥9

Ruff the third heart and cash the ♦A. Why give partner problems? Strange things happen when you don't take charge when you should. Here, partner might try a fourth heart hoping to promote ♠Jxx in your hand or even lead a club in the hope of getting a ruff. Those prematurely gray haired players you see around are the ones who didn't ruff the third heart and are still waiting for a diamond return.

MISCELLANEOUS

289. When you are sure partner has nothing to contribute to the defense, don't make honest discards or signals. Why help declarer?

290. Plan your discards in advance. Be nonchalant when blanking an honor. Don't alert declarer to your problem with hesitations, moans or other obvious signs of distress.

291* Tis better to blank an honor in a key suit than to discard the setting trick in an established suit. Courage.

Both sides vul.
Dealer South

North (dummy)
♠ QJ109
♥ AKQ3
♦ J4
♣ 1064

West (you)
♠ 3
♥ J982
♦ Q10532
♣ K52

East
♠ 87542
♥ 106
♦ K98
♣ 873

South
♠ AK6
♥ 754
♦ A76
♣ AQJ9

South	West	North	East
1♣	Pass	1♥	Pass
2NT	Pass	4NT	All Pass

Opening lead: ♦3

Declarer wins the third diamond and rattles off four spades discarding a heart. What three discards should you make? As soon as partner turns up with the ♦K, you can count declarer for all the missing high cards including the ♣AQJ. As you cannot afford to discard a heart, and discarding more than one diamond allows declarer to set up the club suit, unload two clubs and a diamond.

Neither side vul.
Dealer North

North (dummy)
♠ 105
♥ A43
♦ 7643
♣ AKJ10

West (you)
♠ AQ9832
♥ 10
♦ Q109
♣ 873

North	**East**	**South**	**West**
1♣	Pass	1♥	2♠
Pass	Pass	2NT	All Pass

Opening lead: ♠8

Partner's jack loses to the king. Declarer, holding ♣ Qxx rattles off four club tricks, partner discarding an encouraging heart and declarer a heart as well. What do you discard? Do NOT discard a spade. You must assume partner has another spade and you need to take FIVE spade tricks when partner gets in. Discard a diamond. If declarer has the ♦AKJ, 2NT cannot be beaten and declarer would have bid 3NT, not 2NT, with 13 HCP outside of hearts. Partner must have a high honor in diamonds.

Declarer's hand: ♠ K76 ♥ QJ76 ♦ A52 ♣ Q92
Partner's hand: ♠ J4 ♥ K9852 ♦ KJ8 ♣ 654

292. When declarer has all the tricks but one and there are two suits to be saved, make a clear discard telling partner which suit you are saving so she can save the other.

293. Versus notrump, a discard of your last card in partner's strong suit indicates no hand entry; with an entry there are no words to describe the discard.

294. When you have no important message to send partner and can afford to make a discard from a suit in which declarer already knows your holding, do so.

295. Don't discard winners to keep losers. Don't laugh; players do this all the time.

North (dummy)
Q109632

West
J54

East
K87

South
A

Playing no trump, South cashes the ace and then shifts to another suit. If there are not enough dummy entries to set up this suit, each defender can afford to discard once from this suit.

296. When dummy has shortness and declarer draws trump, the inference is that declarer has no losers to ruff. Therefore, discards in dummy's short suit are safe.

Both sides vul.
Dealer South

North (dummy)
♠ 97432
♥ Q8765
♦ 2
♣ 109

West (you)
♠ 1065
♥ AK43
♦ J1075
♣ 32

East
♠ QJ
♥ 1092
♦ 98432
♣ 654

South
♠ AK8
♥ J
♦ AKQ
♣ AKQJ87

South	West	North	East
2♣	Pass	2♦*	Pass
3♣	Pass	3♦**	Pass
6♣	All Pass		

*Waiting ** Double negative
Opening lead: ♥K

Partner's ♥2 along with declarer's bidding marks declarer with a singleton heart. At trick two you shift to a trump and declarer rattles off six trump winners forcing you to make four discards. Since declarer did not try to ruff a diamond in dummy, diamond discards are safe. Your two small hearts are safe. Your ACE of hearts is safe. What isn't safe is a spade.

297* When holding an inescapable winner in dummy's long suit, holding up to get an informative discard is a clever tactic.

Both sides vul.
Dealer South

North (dummy)
♠ 43
♥ 43
♦ AJ6
♣ QJ10986

West
♠ J9862
♥ AJ103
♦ 75
♣ 75

East (you)
♠ Q107
♥ K62
♦ Q984
♣ K32

South
♠ AK5
♥ Q987
♦ K1032
♣ A4

South	West	North	East
1NT	Pass	3NT	All Pass

Opening lead: ♠6

Declarer wins the opening lead with the ♠K and plays ace and a club. Rather than guess whether to return a spade or a heart, duck the trick. Upon winning the next club, watch partner's discard like a hawk. In this case partner will discard a spade indicating heart strength, so shift to a low heart. Had partner discarded a heart, you would have returned a spade.

298* Declarer's choice of discards from dummy can be revealing.
(1) Any discard from dummy denies a card combination inconsistent with the discard. If declarer discards from AQxx in dummy, declarer won't have Kx(x), but may have Kxxx or no king.
(2) Discards from strong suits (AKJx(x) or AQJx(x)) deny the missing honor.
(3) Discarding down to a void in dummy usually denies the ace in declarer's hand.
(4) Discarding from a small doubleton denies any holding where declarer may have to lead the suit twice to take two finesses, (AQJ(x), KQx(x), KJx(x)).

299. Declarer's discards from her own hand can be revealing. If dummy tables with Qx, Kx or Ax and declarer makes a discard or two from that suit, it is unlikely that declarer has both of the missing honors.

300. A well-known declarer ploy when holding all the tricks but one, and having several discards available, is to make her first discard(s) in the suit she is hoping you abandon. Beware!

301. When dummy has the AKQ in an unbid suit and declarer does not fall all over herself to take discard(s) either:
(1) There is no rush to take the discards.
(2) Declarer has equal or greater length in the suit and no discards are available.

302* Killing a discard or an eventual discard is usually a winning defense.

Both sides vul.
Dealer **West**

North (dummy)
♠ Q832
♥ K54
♦ 873
♣ K86

West (you)
♠ AK975
♥ A
♦ J52
♣ J1093

East
♠ J6
♥ 7632
♦ Q1064
♣ 752

South
♠ 104
♥ QJ1098
♦ AK9
♣ AQ4

West	**North**	**East**	**South**
1♠	Pass	Pass	Dbl.
Pass	1NT	Pass	2♥
Pass	3♥	Pass	4♥
All Pass			

Opening lead: ♠A (A from AK)

When partner starts a high-low, continue with the king and a spade. Assume declarer inserts the eight, ruffed and overruffed. When you win the ♥A, play a fourth spade killing any spade discard once and for all. Eventually you will take the setting trick in diamonds.

303. Discarding a potentially valuable spot card to show strength in a suit in which declarer has inescapable losers puts you back in Pre-K.

(8) GETTING A HANDLE ON DECLARER'S STRENGTH

Knowing approximately how strong a hand declarer has makes the defense that much easier. As the play develops and declarer shows some or all of her strength, your job is to keep track. Sooner or later you should be able to figure out who has what in the middle or end game, hopefully sooner!

BASICS

304. When dummy tables, add declarer's ESTIMATED high-card points (HCP) to the number you see in dummy and subtract from 40. This tells you to within one or two points what the defense is working with. Subtract your HCP from the total and you will know (within a point or two) how strong partner is.

305. Another way to zero in on declarer's strength is to use PARTNER'S bidding, if revealing enough, as a guide

West	**North**	**East** (you)	**South**
Pass	Pass	Pass	1♥
Dbl.	4♥	All Pass.	

Partner's passed hand takeout double shows 9-11 HCP. Add partner's average count (10) to your count and dummy's count, subtract from 40 and presto, you know declarer's strength to within one point.

FROM THE BIDDING (RANGES)

306. Whatever declarer's range, that range narrows if there has been an invitational sequence.

South	**North**
1NT (15-17)	2♣
2♠	2NT
Pass	

When a player with a three point range declines an invitation, assume the lowest count. Play South for 15 HCP.

307. Whenever declarer's (or PARTNER'S) bidding has shown a three point range and there has not been an invitational sequence, assume the middle count.

South	**North**
1NT	3NT
Pass	

If South is playing 15-17, assume 16; if South is playing 16-18, assume 17. Once done, you will know PARTNER'S strength to within one point as soon as dummy appears.

308. When declarer's bidding has shown a four point range assume the two lower counts if an invitation is refused; the two higher if it has been accepted.

South	West	North	East
1♣	Pass	1♥	Pass
1NT	Pass	2NT	Pass
All Pass			

If North-South are playing a one notrump opening range of 16-18, South's range is 12-15, play South for 12-13.

309. When declarer's bidding has shown a five point range assume the two lower counts if an invitation has been refused, the MIDDLE of the three higher if it has been accepted.

North	South
Pass	1♥
1NT (6-10)	2NT
(1) Pass	
(2) 3NT	

In (1) play South for 6-7 HCP, possibly 5.
In (2) play South for the middle count, 9.

310. When responder makes a NON-FORCING jump after a ONE level response, the range varies from 9+ to 12 HCP. (Hands with long suits can invite with as few as 9 HCP).

(1) Opener	Responder	(2) Opener	Responder
1♦	1♥	1♦	1♥
1♠	3♥ (9-11)	1♠, 2♣	2NT (10-12)

Note: some play that ALL second round jumps by the responder are forcing. Ask.

311. Assume a minimum of 12 HCP for an opening bid, but drop that count to 11 if opener shows a distributional hand. If opener rebids the same suit three times without jumping, 10 HCP now becomes a ballpark figure.

312. Assume 16-18 HCP when an opponent makes a takeout double and then bids a major suit after the doubler's partner makes a minimum response.

313. When the opponents use Blackwood and stop at the five level, assume TWO aces are missing. However, if the opponents play Roman Key Card Blackwood, ONE ace plus either the king or queen of trump may be missing.

314. A 3NT response to a minor suit opening bid shows the same strength as a one notrump opening bid. A 3NT response to a major suit opening bid, if not artificial (it almost always is), shows the same strength, (16-17 HCP).

315. Whatever declarer's range, assume the lowest count possible when dummy comes down stronger than expected. If dummy comes down weaker than expected, assume declarer is at the top of her range and work it out from there.

INFERENCES FROM THE PLAY AT TRICK ONE

316. After working out declarer's approximate point count from the bidding, the next step is to determine exactly how much of that strength is in the suit that has been led.

(a)

North (dummy)
J64

West (you)
KQ105

You lead the king which holds. Partner figures to have the ace. If declarer had the ace, it would be normal to win the ace with the jack in the dummy—and don't forget trying to clock in on the important intermediate cards while you're at it.

(b)

North (dummy)
AJ3

West (you)
10862

You lead low, dummy plays the jack, partner the queen and declarer the king. Play partner for the nine. With K9(x)(x), declarer would have played low from dummy.

(c)

North (dummy)
A76

West
Q

East (you)
K10832

Partner leads the Q and dummy plays low, play partner for the jack. With Jxx, declarer would have played dummy's ace.

(d) **North** (dummy)
9843

West (you)
KQJ5

Vs. notrump the lead of the king holds. It is safe to continue with the five as partner is marked with either the ace, the ten, or both. With A10x(x), declarer would have taken the first trick ensuring two tricks in the suit.

Neither side vul.
Dealer North

North (dummy)
♠ 8743
♥ K5
♦ 654
♣ AKQ3

West (you)
♠ J9
♥ Q1072
♦ AQ10
♣ 9842

North	**East**	**South**	**West**
1♣	Pass	1♠	Pass
2♠	Pass	3♠	All Pass

Opening lead: ♥2

Partner tops dummy's king and switches to the ♦9. Declarer plays the jack and you win the queen. Now what? Lead a heart to partner's jack (if declarer had the ♥J, she would have played a low heart at trick one), and wait for another diamond return. With this defense you win the first five tricks before declarer can take breath one. Be sure to congratulate your partner for making TWO good defensive plays; (1) not cashing the jack of hearts prematurely, (saving it for a reentry to lead a second diamond); (2) leading a HIGH diamond to show weakness rather than a lazy fourth best deuce.

Declarer's hand: ♠ AQ652 ♥ 8743 ♦ KJ7 ♣ 4
Partner's hand: ♠ K10 ♥ AJ9 ♦ 9832 ♣ 10765

Against any other defense, declarer pitches two diamonds on the clubs and makes the hand easily.

317. Versus notrump assume the lead of the queen is from top of a sequence. Although there are other possibilities, (AQJxx, KQ109(x), the sequence lead is far and away the most likely.

Neither side vul.
Dealer North

North (dummy)
♠ KQJ109
♥ AKJ
♦ 98
♣ Q109

East (you)
♠ A5
♥ Q75
♦ 652
♣ KJ432

North	**East**	**South**	**West**
1♠	Pass	1NT	Pass
2NT	All Pass		

Opening lead: ♦Q

Declarer wins the king and leads a spade to the king and ace, partner playing the deuce. What now? Declarer has passed 2NT indicating 6-7 HCP and has already turned up with 7 HCP in diamonds. Who has the ♣A? Go straight to the head of the class if you shifted to a low club. Additionally, partner's first spade should be suit preference, not count; count is irrelevant in spades.

Declarer's hand: ♠ 43 ♥ 9863 ♦ AK43 ♣ 876
Partner's hand: ♠ 8762 ♥ 1042 ♦ QJ107 ♣ A5

318. When declarer makes an unnatural play from dummy, look at it with a jaundiced eye.

(a) **North** (dummy)
AQ10

West
2

East (you)
865

Vs. suit, partner's lead of the deuce is taken by the ace. Strange. Unless declarer immediately discards losers in this suit, play declarer for the king.

(b) **North** (dummy)
KJ

West
2

East (you)
A83

Partner leads low vs suit and declarer plays the king. Strange. The lead has marked you with the ace so if declarer is lacking both the queen and ace, the normal play from dummy is the jack. Play declarer for the queen.

(c) **North** (dummy)
Q6

West (you)
108743

You lead low and partner's jack loses to the ace. Strange. Play declarer for the king. If declarer had Ax(x), she would have played the queen from dummy.

(d) **North** (dummy)
K65

West (you)
Q1032

You lead low and dummy's king wins the trick. Play declarer for the ace (good thinking), and partner for the jack. If declarer had the AJx(x), declarer would have played low from dummy.

319. The weaker the declarer's hand, the easier to zero in on her strength. If declarer has a range of 6-8 HCP and turns up with an early AK, play partner for any missing A,K or Q.

INFERENCES FROM THE LATER PLAY

320. When declarer leaves a strong suit (KQJxx, AQJxx) untouched, assume declarer, not partner, has the missing honor. Strong suits missing one key honor are usually attacked early.

Both sides vul.
Dealer South

North (dummy)
♠ 632
♥ Q84
♦ A75
♠ KQJ10

East (you)
♠ 754
♥ KJ75
♦ K102
♣ 765

South	**West**	**North**	**East**
1NT	Pass	3NT	All Pass

Opening lead: **♠J** (J denies)

Declarer wins the ♠Q and runs the ♦J to your ♦K. What now?

Here it helps to be playing "jack denies" since it tells you that declarer has three spade tricks as well as 9HCP in spades. (On other hands the information helps declarer more). Declarer's failure to attack clubs places her with the ace and four more tricks. In addition, the play of the ♦J reeks of the queen since you are looking at the ♦10. Are you beginning to get the picture? Declarer has 16 HCP plus nine tricks OUTSIDE of hearts. Switch to a low heart and rake in the tricks.

Declarer's hand: ♠ AKQ ♥ 1032 ♦ QJ94 ♣ A43
Partner's hand: ♠ J1098 ♥ A96 ♦ 863 ♣ 982

321. As the play develops and either declarer or partner can have an important missing honor, but partner needs the honor to defeat the contract, be a sport and play partner for the honor.

North (dummy)
QJ107

West (you)
K6

This is a side suit vs. a suit contract and you are on lead holding worthless trump. If you need partner to have the ace to defeat the contract, swing the king. If you can defeat the contract even if declarer has the ace, lead something else.

(9)
ZEROING IN ON DECLARER'S DISTRIBUTION

It is important to get an EARLY count on declarer's hand. You have five guideposts to help you:

(1) The opponents' bidding.
(2) Partner's bidding.
(3) Partner's leads and count signals.
(4) Inferences from the play.
(5) Declarer's and partner's show-outs.

BASICS

322. The better your opponents bid, the more you can rely on their bidding to help you work out declarer's hand pattern. Be wary of drawing normal bidding inferences from weak, inexperienced, or exasperated opponents.

323. Use the opponents' bidding agreements to help you: i.e, five card majors, negative doubles, Flannery, or any two-suited overcalls (Michaels, Unusual Notrump, etc.). Don't hesitate to ask questions if those agreements are not written.

INFERENCES FROM THE OPENER'S BIDDING

324. Most inferences are drawn from the bids that the opponents do NOT make. For example, if the opponents are playing Flannery an opening bid of 2♦ shows five hearts and four spades (11-15 HCP). If opener bids 1♥ and turns up with more than 15 HCP, she may have four spades, if she turns up with a minimum, assume fewer than four spades.

325. After a 1♦ opening and a 1♥ response, if opener does not rebid spades, assume the opener does not have four spades. However, if opener jumps to 2NT, this assumption is not valid. (See tip 342)

326. If an opening 1♦ bidder does not raise a major suit response directly, play opener for at least four diamonds.

327. When an opening 1♠ bidder does not rebid hearts, assume fewer than four hearts. However, if opener rebids spades at a minimum level and then bids hearts, assume 6-4. If opener rebids anything other than 2♠ and then bids hearts on the third round of bidding, play opener for three hearts.

(a)

Opener	Responder
1♠	1NT
2♠	2NT
3♥ (6-4)	

(b)

Opener	Responder
1♠	1NT
2♣	2NT
3♥	(5-3-1-4)

328. When the opener skips over three bids (two suits and notrump) to rebid her first suit, assume she has six.

Opener	Responder
1♥	1♠
2♥ (six hearts)	

Opener skipped over 1NT, 2♣ and 2♦.

329. When opener rebids her original suit bypassing FEWER than three bids, she may have five or six.

Opener	Responder
1♥	2♣ or 2♦
2♥ (five or six hearts)	

However, if two over one is a game force and a 2NT rebid by the opener shows a minimum, chances are greater that opener has a a six card heart suit.

330. When opener bids a second suit and then rebids the first suit, assume a strong 6-4 hand.

(a)

Opener	Responder
1♥	1♠
2♣	2NT
3♥	4♥

(b)

Opener	Responder
1♥	1♠
2♥	2NT
3♦	Pass

In (a) opener shows six hearts and four clubs, forcing.
In (b) opener shows six hearts and four diamonds, not forcing.

331. When an opening 1♦ bidder turns up with three diamonds, the most likely distribution is 4-4 in the majors with a doubleton club-NO SINGLETONS, NO FIVE CARD SUITS .

332. When an opening 1♣ bidder turns up with three clubs and two diamonds, opener must be 4-4 in the majors.

333. When an opening 1♣ bidder turns up with three clubs and three diamonds, opener must be 4-3 or 3-4 in the majors.

334. When an opening 1♣ bidder turns up with three clubs and four diamonds, assume the opener doesn't know how to bid.

335. Make normal counting inferences during the bidding. Do not try to be a genius. (Assume a second suit is four cards long until proven otherwise, etc.).

336. Three level jump rebids tend to show six card suits; four level jump rebids, seven card suits.

Opener	Responder
1♥	1♠
3♥ (usually six hearts, could be seven)	
4♥ (usually seven hearts, could be six)	

337. When opener reverses, assume 5-4 in the two suits. If opener makes a third bid, more definitive distributional information is available.

Opener	**Responder**	**Opener**	**Responder**	**Opener**	**Responder**
1♣	1♠	1♣	1♠	1♣	1♠
2♥ (5-4)		2♦	2♥	2♥	2NT
		3♣ (6-4)		3♠ (3-4-1-5)	

338. If opener bids the higher ranking of TOUCHING suits and then rebids a lower ranking suit twice, assume 5-5 but allow for 6-5 or even 5-6 with less than reversing strength.

Opener	Responder
1♥	1♠
2♦	2NT
3♦	

Play opener for 5-5 or 6-5 either way. If opener has five hearts and six diamonds, opener must be minimum. Requirements for a reverse with 5-6 distribution dip to as low as 13-14 HCP when the strength is concentrated in the two long suits.

339. If opener bids the higher ranking of NON-TOUCHING suits and then rebids a lower ranking suit twice, assume 5-5 or 6-5, opener's first suit longer. It is rare to open one spade with five spades and six diamonds or one heart with five hearts and six clubs; opening the lower ranking suit is the normal action.

Opener	Responder
1♠	2♣
2♦	2NT
3♦	

Assume opener is 5-5, perhaps 6-5, spades longer. It would be rare, but not impossible, to open 1♠ with five spades and six diamonds. Perhaps: ♠ AKQJ9 ♥ 2 ♦ Q87432 ♣ 4

340. When the opponents preempt, take a look at the vulnerability. If you are vulnerable and they are not, subtract one card from the normal expected length.

341. Play a vulnerable 4-level preemptive bidder to have either an eight card suit or a 7-4 hand. A non-vulnerable 4-level preempt may be based on only a seven card suit, particularly when your side is vulnerable. (See previous tip).

342. A jump rebid to 2NT after a minor suit opening bid does NOT deny a four card major.

Opener	Responder
1♣	1♦

2NT (could have one (or two!) four card majors).

343. In the modern game a jump rebid of 3NT after a one level response shows an UNBALANCED HAND, typically a solid six or seven card minor with shortness in responder's suit.

Opener	Responder
1♣	1♠
3NT	

Opener may hold: ♠ 5 ♥ KJ5 ♦ K4 ♣ AKQ9865

344. DELAYED support shows THREE cards; direct support of a first bid suit, three OR four cards. (Some promise four card support when giving direct support).

Opener	Responder
1♠ (5)	2♣
2♥ (4)	2NT
3♣ (3)	3♠
4♠	Pass

Opener is probably playing a 5-2 fit.

345. If the opponents play "support" doubles, distributional inferences are available.

South	**West**	**North**	**East**
1♦	Pass	1♠	2♥
Dbl, 2♠			

Playing support doubles, South's double of 2♥ shows three spades, a direct raise shows four. If responder bids beyond the two level in spades, assume responder has five or more spades. If opener becomes the declarer, you know she has three spades.

If opener neither doubles nor supports spades, play opener for fewer than three spades.

346. When opener shows a balanced hand, her most common distribution is 4-4-3-2 (ANY 4-4-3-2). Begin by assuming she has that pattern as opposed to ANY 4-3-3-3 or ANY 5-3-3-2 pattern.

347. Once a known balanced hand turns up with a five card suit, the trick is to sniff out the doubleton. Once done, you can be reasonably sure that declarer is 3-3 in the two other suits.

Opener	Responder
1♠	2♣
2NT	3♣
3NT	Pass

Opener rates to be 5-3-3-2 with a likely doubleton club.

348. When the opponents use Stayman, a bundle of distributional information becomes available.

(a)

Opener	Responder
1NT	2♣
2♦	3NT
Pass	

(b)

Opener	Responder
1NT	2♣
2♥	3NT
Pass	

(c)

Opener	Responder
1NT	2♣
2♦	3♥,3♠
3NT	Pass

(d)

Opener	Responder
1NT	2♣
2♥	3NT
4♠	Pass

In (a) opener denies a four card major. If opener turns up with a doubleton in one minor, assume five cards in the other. If opener turns up with a doubleton in one major, play opener for three cards in the other. AN OPENING NOTRUMP BIDDER IS UNLIKELY TO HAVE TWO DOUBLETONS. However, if the notrump bidder shows up with a six card minor (rare) assume 6-3-2-2 distribution.

In (b) if opener turns up with a doubleton club (say), play opener for three spades and four diamonds. With four spades, opener would have bid 4♠ over 3NT.

In (c) responder shows a five card major and opener's 3NT rebid tends to indicate a doubleton in that major. In addition, opener has denied four cards in the other major. Assume opener is 3-2 in the majors. Once you get a count on one minor, the whole hand counts out.

In (d) opener has two four card majors and must be 4-4-3-2 or 4-4-2-3.

349. When the opponents play Jacoby, distributional information is available. LISTEN.

Opener	Responder
1NT	2♦ (Transfer to hearts)
2♥,2NT,3♥	

The 2♥ bid can show two or three hearts, seldom four. A 2NT rebid shows three hearts with a maximum (some play two of the top three honors); the leap to 3♥, as most play, shows four hearts.

Opener	Responder
1NT	2♦ (shows five hearts)
2♥	3♣ (natural)
3NT	

Play opener for a doubleton heart. If opener turns up with five diamonds, play opener for 3-2-5-3.

WHEN PARTNER BIDS

350. When partner makes a two-suited overcall, counting declarer's hand becomes much easier. The bad news is that declarer can count your hand(s) easier, too.

(a)

South	**West**	**North**	**East** (you)
1♥	2NT*	4♥	All Pass

* Minors

You start by knowing partner is 5-5 or 6-5 in the minors. Looking at your hand and the dummy, you can calculate declarer's minor suit length. Once you can nail down one of the major suits, you have a pretty good count on the hand.

(b)

South	**West**	**North**	**East** (you)
1♦	2♦*	3♦	Pass
3NT	All Pass		

* Michaels

Partner usually has 5-5 in the majors (sometimes 4-5), so that is a good start.

INFERENCES FROM THE RESPONDER'S BIDDING

351. Be wary of a 1♥ or 1♠ response to a 1♣ opening. If responder has exactly four cards in the major, a longer diamond suit may be lurking in the bushes. If the opponents have any agreements about diamond concealment, you should be alerted.

352. A two level response in hearts or a two level competitive response in either hearts or spades guarantees a five card suit, minimum; a two level response in a minor can be made on a four bagger.

(a)

Opener	Responder
1♠	2♣, 2♦ (can be made with a four card suit).
1♠	2♥ (promises at least five hearts).

(b)

South	**West**	**North**
1♦	2♣	2♥, 2♠ (promises at least five cards).

353. A 1NT response to a major suit opening bid does not necessarily show a balanced hand. The responder may have a wildly unbalanced hand that is not strong enough to make a two level response. Responder might even be void in opener's major. Be ready for anything.

354. Natural, initial, jump responses of 2NT or 3NT show balanced hands; REBIDS of 2NT or 3NT by the responder, may not. Some play the direct jump to 2NT or 3NT after a minor suit opening denies a four card major; others do not. ASK.

(a)

Opener	Responder
1♦	2NT, 3NT
Pass	

(b)

Opener	Responder
1♦	2♣
2♦	2NT, 3NT
	Pass

In (a) responder is balanced; in (b) responder could have six clubs and a singleton diamond.

355. It is very important to know declarer's trump length as early as possible. Use their bidding agreements to help you.

Opener	Responder
1♣	1♥
2♥	4♥
Pass	

If opener PROMISES four hearts, responder can have four; if opener can have three hearts, play responder for at least five.

356. If responder rebids notrump after her one level major suit response has been supported, play responder for four cards in the major.

Opener	Responder
1♦	1♥
2♥	2NT (responder shows four hearts)
3♥	Pass

357. When the response to 1♣ or 1♦ is 1♠ and the responder turns up with four spades, assume responder has fewer than four hearts.

358. A ONE level negative double promises four cards in the unbid major(s). If the negative doubler later bids a major, play the negative doubler for a five card major.

South	**West**	**North**	**East**
1♣	1♦	Dbl.*	2♦
Pass	Pass	2♥	

* Negative

Play North for five hearts and four spades.

359. Playing negative doubles, a 1♠ response after a 1♥ overcall shows five spades, minimum; with four, responder doubles.

South	**West**	**North**	**East**
1♣	1♥	Dbl. (shows four spades)	
1♣	1♥	1♠ (shows five or more spades)	

Some play that the double denies four spades, ASK.

360. Experienced responders usually rebid six card suits, not five card suits unless the suit is very strong or they have been forced to make a rebid.

(a)	Opener	Responder
	1♥	1♠
	2♣	2♠

Since the 2♣ rebid is not forcing, play responder for six spades.

(b)	Opener	Responder
	1♣	1♠
	2♥	2♠ (five or six spades)

Since two hearts is forcing and responder must bid something, the 2♠ rebid does not necessarily promise a six card suit.

361. When responder bids the fourth suit and later becomes declarer, there is NO inference that responder has length in the fourth suit; responder frequently uses the fourth suit to create a force.

Opener	Responder
1♥	1♠
2♣	2♦ (fourth suit)
2♠	4♠

Impossible to gauge responder's diamond length.

ADVANCED COMPETITIVE BIDDING INFERENCES

362* When you overcall and partner, marked with some strength, does not support, play partner for fewer than three cards in your suit.

363* When partner fails to compete to the three level after you have raised a presumed five card suit, play partner for a five card suit; with a six card suit, three level competition is quasi-mandatory.

South	**West**	**North**	**East** (you)
1♥	1♠	2♥	2♠
Pass	Pass	3♥	All Pass

Play partner for five spades and declarer for five hearts. If either player had a six card major it would have been normal to compete to the three level.

364* When a player competes to the three level after having PUSHED the opponents to the three level and turns up with five trump (knowing only of three card support), assume she has a side four card suit. Strong players seldom "take the push" to the three level with 5-3-3-2 distribution.

365* After partner opens the bidding and you make a negative double showing length in the unbid major(s), play partner for fewer than four cards in either major if partner fails to compete in that major(s) at the one or two level.

East	**South**	**West** (you)	**North**
1♣	1♦	Dbl.*	2♦
All Pass			

* Negative, presumably showing both majors.

Play partner for fewer than four hearts or four spades, play declarer for five diamonds. Now with a count signal here and a show-out there, you've got it.

366. When partner makes a takeout double and then raises your FORCED response in the teeth of strong competitive bidding, play partner for four trump plus a likely singleton.

MYSTERY SUITS

367. Try to develop the habit of adding your length to dummy's length in "mystery" (unbid) suits. Subtract the total from 13 and then try to decide how the remaining cards are divided between the two unseen hands. (It's actually fun!)

368* If partner has led from a known four card suit (notrump), and you can see four cards between you and dummy in another (unbid) suit, assume declarer has five and partner four cards in this suit. Holding five cards in the suit, partner would probably have led the suit. However, if the bidding suggests that declarer cannot have five, play partner for five. STAY FLEXIBLE.

369. If partner has been in the bidding and you can see five cards between you and dummy in an UNBID MAJOR, assume the suit is divided 4-4. Surely the suit would have been mentioned if either player had a five card suit.

370. A Weak Two bid in one major usually denies four cards in the other major. Use this tip to help you count declarer's hand. A Weak 2♦ opening bid usually denies four cards in either major.

371. When your opponents end up in notrump or in a minor suit contract, assume they do not have an eight card or longer major suit fit. This may help you infer declarer's major suit distribution.

372. When you can see 10 cards between your hand and dummy in an unbid suit and partner leads something else, assume declarer, not partner, has the shortness. Not many partners can resist leading a singleton in an unbid suit. However, if partner is the one that turns up with the singleton, play partner for a strong trump holding.

373* With an inference here and an inference there, you can get an inferential count.

East-West vul. **North** (dummy)
Dealer West
♠ J65
♥ AJ5
♦ K943
♣ 943

East (you)
♠ K103
♥ 874
♦ QJ872
♣ 106

West	**North**	**East**	**South**
1♣	Pass	1♦	1♥
2♣	2♥	All Pass	

Opening lead: ♦10

What do you know? Partner cannot have four spades and is a heavy favorite to have SIX clubs. Declarer is likely to have five hearts and cannot have five spades. Voila, South is 4-5-2-2 and partner is 3-2-2-6.

374* Accurate counting comes with practice. Use every hand you defend as a practice board until you get the hang of it. Here's a chance to show off.

Both sides vul.
Dealer South

North (dummy)
♠ K1054
♥ 64
♦ KQ654
♣ Q7

East (you)
♠ A987
♥ J
♦ AJ2
♣ 109854

South	**West**	**North**	**East**
1♦	2♥*	Dbl.**	Pass
2♠	Pass	3♠	All Pass

* Weak Jump Overcall
** Negative Double

Opening lead: ♣2 (fourth best).

What is the exact distribution around the table?

Start from square one. Partner is marked with six hearts leaving South four. South should have four spades (no reason for South to bid a three card spade suit holding four hearts to some high honor(s), given the non-heart lead. So South is 4-4 in the majors with five minor suit cards. South can't have four diamonds as that would give partner five clubs, impossible from the lead. Ergo, **South** is 4-4-3-2 and partner has probably blown a trick by leading away from the ♣K. What else is new?

GIVING AND GETTING COUNT SIGNALS

Besides the help you get from the bidding, there is more on the way—partner's count signals. Good partners know when to give, and, equally important, when NOT to give count.

375* When declarer starts a side suit, watch for partner's signals. Do not expect (or give) honest count if declarer's length is known from the bidding. COUNT SIGNALS ARE FOR MYSTERY SUITS, NOT KNOWN SUITS.

	North (dummy)	
	84	
West (you)		**East**
J96		Q1053
	South	
	AK72	

Assume this is a side suit in a suit contract and South is known to have four cards in the suit. East-West should not give count, they already know it.

376* Do NOT give count:

(1) When declarer's length is known.
(2) When you have all the missing strength.
(3) When playing with a partner who doesn't count.
(4) When count is irrelevant and suit preference is far more important.

377*

377* Declarer seldom attacks equally divided suits early in the play. If declarer begins by leading a doubleton from the dummy, bet big bucks declarer doesn't have a doubleton as well. Ditto when declarer starts a three card suit from dummy.

East-West vul.
Dealer West

North (dummy)
♠ J986
♥ QJ6
♦ A72
♣ K86

West
♠ K742
♥ 52
♦ 1053
♣ AQ92

East (you)
♠ AQ1053
♥ 83
♦ KQ9
♣ 753

South
♠ -
♥ AK10974
♦ J864
♣ J104

West	North	East	South
Pass	Pass	1♠	2♥
3♠	4♥	All Pass	

Opening lead: ♠2

Declarer ruffs the opening lead, draws two trump ending in dummy and leads a low diamond to your queen, partner flagging an odd number. It should be clear that declarer has four diamonds and is trying to set up a fourth diamond for a club discard from dummy. Your counter is to attack clubs at once. Switch to a high club. Assume declarer plays the jack. Partner must play the queen to drive out the king. Later when in with your ♦K, you can return another club for down one.

378* If you know from the bidding that the opponents hold the AKQ of a suit, do not give count if a third round finesse against a ten or jack is possible.

North (dummy)
Q1076

West (you)
J932

East
54

South
AK8

If declarer is marked with the ace-king, do not give count from either side.

379. When marked with SHORTNESS, playing the highest missing card under a winner indicates it is your last card in the suit. Don't get too tricky with equals; it throws partner off the count.

North (dummy)
9732

West (you)
QJ4

East
108

South
AK65

When declarer plays ace-king, play low-jack, not low-queen. If you play low-queen, partner may think declarer has a five card suit and misdefend. If she does, it is on your head.

380* When marked with LENGTH, playing the highest missing card on the third round of the suit tells partner that declarer is out of the suit.

North (dummy)
105

West
J32

East (you)
Q9864

South
AK7

When declarer plays the AK and ruffs the seven, your play of the queen on the third round announces that either you or declarer is out of the suit. Because there is a two card differential, partner is expected to work it out.

381. When ANYONE shows out, the count is known. If you still have trouble counting when someone shows out, it is time to review the common hand patterns —out loud! Do not do this around non-bridge players. They think we are crazy enough as it is.

382. Once you have a count on two suits, ask yourself how many cards declarer has in the two remaining suits. Now go back to the bidding and partner's lead(s) and/or count signal(s) to work out the mystery. You can do it!

383. Counting comes in particularly handy when declarer is stripping the hand preparing for a throw-in or eventually getting around to playing that last critical suit.

East-West vul.
Dealer North

North (dummy)
♠ J109
♥ 765
♦ AQ954
♣ K9

East (you)
♠ 7653
♥ AK93
♦ 73
♣ QJ10

North	East	South	West
Pass	Pass	1♦	Pass
3♦	Pass	5♦	All Pass

Opening lead: ♠K

Declarer wins, crosses the ♦Q; ruffs a spade; returns to the♦A, partner discarding a spade, and ruffs dummy's last spade. Are you counting? Declarer continues with a club to the king, partner playing the deuce, a club to the ace and a club ruff in dummy. Finally, a heart is led from dummy. What is declarer's distribution and which heart do you play?

Declarer is marked with 1-4-5-3 and since you need THREE heart tricks to defeat the contract, play low so as not to block the suit in case partner has the needed Jx or Qx.

Declarer's hand: ♠ A ♥ Q1042 ♦ KJ1082 ♣ A76
Partner's hand: ♠ KQ842 ♥ J8 ♦ 6 ♠ 85432

PARTNER'S LEADS AND RETURNS—MORE COUNT INFORMATION

384. Watch (and draw inferences from) partner's carding starting at trick one. Major league misery is around the corner if you don't.

Both sides vul.
Dealer South

North (dummy)
♠ AJ8
♥ J76
♦ AKQ108
♣ J7

West
♠ 6
♥ K9832
♦ J75
♣ Q432

East (you)
♠ 32
♥ AQ10
♦ 9632
♣ A985

South
♠ KQ109754
♥ 54
♦ 4
♣ K106

South	West	North	East
3♠	Pass	4♠	All Pass

Opening lead: ♥3

Win the opening lead with the ten (partner needs the ♥K to defeat the contract), and continue with the ♥A. When partner plays the ♥2, showing five, shift to a LOW club because you need TWO club tricks to set the contract. Had partner played up the line in hearts, you would cash the ♣A and then lead a third heart.

385* Unless partner is giving you a ruff or thinks she is giving you a ruff, partner's return in your suit is present count. Watch the spots!

East-West vul.
Dealer South

North (dummy)
♠ 104
♥ 104
♦ J94
♣ AJ6543

West (you)
♠ K53
♥ A76
♦ Q1032
♣ K108

South	West	North	East
1♠	Pass	1NT	Pass
2♥	Pass	2♠	All Pass

Opening lead: ♦2

Partner wins the ♦A and returns the ♦8 to declarer's king. At trick two declarer leads the ♣Q. Are you going to cover?

No! Partner's return of a high spot card indicates an original holding of two or three diamonds. If partner has two diamonds, declarer has four, but that is impossible. Declarer is known to have nine cards in the majors and has already played a club. Therefore both partner and declarer have three diamonds and that ♣Q is a singleton. If you duck, declarer cannot get to dummy to enjoy a diamond discard on the ♣J and the contract can be defeated.

Declarer's hand: ♠ AJ982 ♥ QJ95 ♦ K76 ♣ Q
Partner's hand: ♠ Q76 ♥ K832 ♦ A85 ♣ 942

386. If you are into standing ovations, use the count from partner's lead plus declarer's likely distribution from the bidding to make some truly awe-inspiring plays.

Neither side vul.
Dealer South

North (dummy)
♠ 107643
♥ K5
♦ AQ93
♣ 86

East (you)
♠ AJ92
♥ 1074
♦ 1062
♣ A95

South	**West**	**North**	**East**
1♥	Pass	1♠	Pass
2♦	Pass	3♦	Pass
3NT	All Pass		

Opening lead: ♣3

You win the ace and declarer drops the seven. What now? Declarer is marked with nine red cards and must have at least three clubs. Ergo, declarer has at most one spade. Swing the ace, continue with a low spade and wait for the applause.
Declarer's hand: ♠ K ♥ AQ982 ♦KJ54 ♣ KJ7
Partner's hand: ♠ Q85 ♥ J63 ♦ 87 ♣ Q10432

Both sides vul.
Dealer South

North (dummy)
♠ 86
♥ K8
♦ KJ65
♣ A8765

East (you)
♠ 105
♥ A963
♦ A72
♣ KJ93

South	**West**	**North**	**East**
1♠	Pass	2♣	Pass
2♦	Pass	3♦	Pass
3NT	All Pass		

Opening lead: ♥2

Dummy plays low, plan your defense.Judging from the bidding and the opening lead, it is safe to assume that declarer has 5-3-4-1 distribution. Win the ♥A and shift to the ♣K. More applause.

Declarer's hand: ♠ AKQ32 ♥ Q105 ♦ Q1094 ♣ Q
Partner's hand: ♠ J754 ♥ J742 ♦ 83 ♣ 1042

MISCELLANEOUS

387. Distributional assumptions must be consistent with the bidding. For example, if either partner or declarer turns up with a singleton, do not play that hand for a another singleton unless there has been some wild bidding.

388. Holding the ace and seeing KJx(x) in dummy to your left, prepare for the inevitable, declarer leading the suit. Although it is usually right to play low, there are several times when it clearly wrong: (1) when it is the setting trick and can conceivably be lost; (2) when declarer has a singleton and there are no side entries to dummy.

Both sides vul.
Dealer South

North (dummy)
♠ J5
♥ 876
♦ KJ109
♣ J976

West (You)
♠ 82
♥ KQ4
♦ A765
♣ A853

South	**West**	**North**	**East**
3♠	All Pass		

Opening lead: ♥K

You continue with the queen and a heart to partner's jack, declarer following. At trick four partner leads a low club to the king and ace. When you return a club, the nine is played from dummy, partner plays the ten, and declarer ruffs. Declarer exits with a diamond. Are you ready? What do you do?

Play low! Declarer is marked with a 7-3-2-1 hand pattern and you cannot lose your ace even if declarer guesses correctly. However, if declarer misguesses, the hand can be defeated three tricks, vulnerable.

Declarer's hand: ♠ AQ109743 ♥ 1052 ♦ 84 ♣ K
Partner's hand: ♠ K6 ♥ AJ93 ♦ Q32 ♣ Q1042

389. Do not be surprised to discover your game dipping a notch or two when you first start "serious" counting. In fact, it is guaranteed. However, the flip side of the coin is this: once you get the "knack" your game will improve so dramatically that it will be unrecognizable — that is also guaranteed. And you will probably be able to move up to a better class of partner, one who also counts!

(10)
COUNTING DECLARER'S TRICKS — NO TRUMP

Bridge is a game of tricks, yours and theirs. It is far easier for declarer to count her own tricks (she can see dummy), while you and partner have to rely on clear leads and signals to count declarer's tricks. The trick count tells you whether you must defend actively or passively, the crux of (notrump) defense. Also, defenders must keep in mind that when attacking a new suit AFTER trick one, one frequently attacks with a different card than would have been led on opening lead from the same holding.

BASICS

390* When declarer is known to have enough tricks in three suits to make her contract, shift to the fourth suit unless it is CLEARLY wrong. (The most important tip in the chapter).

Neither side vul.
Dealer North

North (dummy)
♠ Q10
♥ K4
♦ AJ10765
♣ AK2

East (you)
♠ KJ42
♥ QJ1073
♦ K4
♣ 96

North	East	South	West
1♦	1♥	1NT	Pass
3NT	Pass	Pass	Pass

Opening lead: ♥8

Declarer wins the opening lead with the ace and runs the diamond queen to your king. Now what? You can see that declarer has nine tricks; five diamonds, two hearts and at least two clubs. Switch to a low spade, it is your ONLY chance.

Declarer's hand (for the curious): ♠ 976 ♥ A965 ♦ Q3 ♣ Q875
Partner's hand (for the lazy): ♠ A853 ♥ 82 ♦ 982 ♣ J1043

391* When you need to put partner in to return your original suit OR the trick count tells you that you must attack another suit, how should poor partner determine which suit to return, your original suit or your second suit?

(1) If you want your FIRST suit returned, switch to a HIGH spot card in the second suit.

(2) If you want your SECOND suit returned, switch to a LOW spot card in your second suit.

THE SUIT THAT HAS BEEN LED

392. Start your trick count in the suit that has been led.

Both sides vul.
Dealer North

North (dummy)
♠ AK2
♥ 843
♦ 43
♣ KQJ104

West (you)
♠ 10983
♥ AQ9
♦ J10982
♣ A

North	**East**	**South**	**West**
1♣	Pass	2NT	Pass
3NT	All Pass		

Opening lead: ♦J

Declarer wins the ♦K, partner playing the ♦5. At trick two a club is led to your ace. Plan your defense. Partner's trick one signal denies an honor so play declarer for the AKQ (three tricks). Once the ♣A is removed, nine tricks are staring you in the face four clubs, three diamonds and two spades. Your only hope is to play partner for ♥Kxxx and shift to the ace or queen of hearts at trick three. As an aside, partner should be able to tell you about heart strength on the club play because count is clearly irrelevant. (See tip 317)

Declarer's hand: ♠ QJ7 ♥ J107 ♦ AKQ ♣ 9765
Partner's hand: ♠ 654 ♥ K652 ♦ 765 ♣ 832

When partner leads a high spot card that cannot logically be fourth best, assume it is top or second high from 9xxx or 10xxx and start counting tricks. (See tip 73)

Both sides vul.
Dealer North

North (dummy)
♠ 763
♥ KQ
♦ K843
♣ AQJ9

East (you)
♠ Q84
♥ 1092
♦ AJ62
♣ 743

North	East	South	West
1♣	Pass	2NT*	Pass
3NT	All Pass		

Opening lead: ♥8

* 13-15 (may have a four card major)

Dummy wins the ♥Q and a low diamond is led. Plan your defense.

It appears from the lead that declarer has four heart tricks and the dummy tells you that four club tricks are available. Do not let declarer sneak that ninth trick by you. Rise with the ace and shift to the ♠ Q like a player.

Declarer's hand: K95 ♥ AJ73 ♦ Q95 ♣ K102
Partner's hand: ♠ AJ102 ♥ 8654 ♦ 107 ♣ 865

394. Even when partner leads an honor, normally indicating a strong holding, count tricks before automatically returning partner's suit.

Both sides vul.
Dealer North

North (dummy)
♠ 97
♥ 873
♦ AKQ109
♣ AJ2

East (you)
♠ 8652
♥ Q104
♦ 762
♣ K109

North	**East**	**South**	**West**
1♦	Pass	2NT	Pass
3NT	All Pass		

Opening lead: ♠Q

Declarer wins the ♠A and leads a club to the jack and king. Your play?

Declarer is known to have two spades, five diamonds and at least two club tricks for a grand total of nine. If this hand is to be beaten it must be in hearts, NOT spades. Shift to the ♥10 and hope partner has ♥AJxx. The lead of the ♥10 does not deny the queen; the lead of the ♥Q does deny the ten.

There is more to this hand than meets the eye, partner's spade holding for one thing. When declarer wins the first trick with the ace there is the fear that partner may have led from KQ109x. Had declarer won the trick with the king, there would be the gnawing possibility that partner has led from AQJxx. It would be nice if partner, instead of giving count, could tell you by the size of her club whether she wanted a spade or a heart returned, wouldn't it? (See tip 572).

Declarer's hand: ♠ AK ♥ K92 ♦ J543 ♣ Q843

Partner's hand: ♠ QJ1043 ♥ AJ65 ♦8 ♣ 765

395* Because the lead of a low card does not tell partner your exact honor strength, you may be able to clarify your strength later by playing your HIGHEST remaining equal on the second round of the suit.

Both sides vul.
Dealer South

North (dummy)
♠ 965
♥ AQ10
♦ KJ8764
♣ A

West (you)
♠ AQ102
♥ 743
♦ 9
♣ J9832

East
♠ J87
♥ K982
♦ 1032
♣ K106

South
♠ K43
♥ J65
♦ AQ5
♣ Q754

South	West	North	East
Pass	Pass	1♦	Pass
2NT	Pass	3NT	All Pass

Opening lead: ♣3

Partner signals with the ten and declarer crosses to the ♦A and leads a heart to the queen and king. When partner plays the ♣K, play the JACK, your highest remaining equal to deny the queen. Forewarned, partner will shift to the ♠J. Down two.

396* Notrump defense is inexorably tied to the number of tricks declarer's or dummy's long suit is likely to produce. Train yourself to guesstimate that number. You have your own holding plus the bidding to help you. However, if partner needs an honor (or a stopper) in the suit to defeat the contract, assume she has it.

(a)

North (dummy)
AK8743

West (you)
95

East
Q106

South
J2

If declarer is balanced, you cannot be sure whether declarer has five or six tricks available. (Declarer can always duck a round). If you need partner to have Qxx to defeat the contract, assume she has it. Partner, on the other hand, counts five EVENTUAL tricks for the declarer.

(b)

North (dummy)
KQ1042

West
986

East (you)
AJ7

South
53

You may have to rely on partner's count card plus the number of side entries to dummy to give you the trick count. Giving standard count, partner must be careful to play SECOND highest from four small if the card can be spared.

In this diagram assume the six is from 986 or (6x). Sometimes the bidding will reveal which, particulary if the suit is a major. In any case, if the queen or king is played from dummy it is almost always right to duck. If the declarer has a doubleton and there is only one side entry to dummy, declarer can only get one trick. If the declarer has three small and you can remove dummy's entry, you can again limit declarer to but one trick.

397* When partner defends passively in the wake of a long suit in dummy, relax, partner has the suit all tied up.

North (dummy)
AQ1087

West (you)
32

East
KJ96

South
54

Although it is impossible for you to tell how many tricks declarer has coming in this suit, partner's defense can serve as guide. If partner defends passively, you should be the one leading the suit!

398* It is far more difficult to count tricks when the long suit is in the concealed hand. However, if declarer makes a strange play from dummy at trick one and/or sets about establishing a trick in your nearly solid suit, Christmas has not arrived. Declarer is out stealing with hidden tricks in the closed hand.

East-West vul.
Dealer West

North (dummy)
♠ QJ10942
♥ 93
♦ K1084
♣ 6

East (you)
♠ A53
♥ AQJ108
♦ J
♣ 8732

West	**North**	**East**	**South**
Pass	2♠	Pass	3NT
All Pass			

Opening lead: ♦6

Declarer wins the king in dummy as you are still berating yourself for not bidding hearts. But low and behold, declarer leads a low heart from dummy at trick two. What is your game plan?

Strange. The trick one play from dummy looks suspicious, and now declarer is tackling hearts. Give me a break. Declarer is stealing. You don't have TIME to set up your hearts, you should be cashing out instead. Win the ♥A and shift to a low spade. Partner clearly has the ♠K and two diamond winners should be over there as well.

Declarer's hand: ♠ - ♥ K65 ♦ 953 ♣ AKQJ1094
Partner's hand: ♠ K872 ♥ 542 ♦ AQ762 ♣ 5

Both sides vul.
Dealer South

North (dummy)
♠ KJ5
♥ 8632
♦ 9765
♣ QJ

West (you)
♠ 107
♥ A104
♦ 832
♣ A10954

South	**West**	**North**	**East**
2NT	Pass	3NT	All Pass

Opening lead: ♣5

Dummy wins the first trick, partner playing the ♣8, count. At trick two declarer leads the ♣Q from dummy, partner following. Plan your defense.

Are you thrilled that declarer has lost her mind and is helping you establish your club suit while you still have an outside entry? Don't be so naive.

Declarer isn't setting up your suit while you still have an outside entry because you are cute. The entry you are cherishing so is probably declarer's weakest suit!

Your play is to win the ♣A and shift to the ♥10 hoping to unblock the suit in case partner has KJ7x or KQ7x. Hats off if you worked this one out. (Of course, partner must play the ♥K from KJ7x when you lead the ten, or else another brilliant play by you goes down the drain).

Declarer's hand: ♠ AQ6 ♥ Q9 ♦ AKQ10 ♣ K763
Partner's hand: ♠ 98432 ♥ KJ75 ♦ J4 ♣ 82

399* Prepare your nervous system for a jolt when dummy tables with an AKJ10x(x) or an AQJx(x)(x) suit and you are sitting in back of this suit with honor doubleton (or honor third); if dummy has no side entry, it is usually right to duck the first trick!

North (dummy)
AKJ102

West
(1) 8643
(2) 864

East (you)
(1) Q5
(2) Q53

South
97

If you have to kill this suit, duck the nine. For all declarer knows, partner has Qxxx. Granted, it is easier to make this ducking play with Kx(x) in back of an AQJx(x)(x) suit as declarer almost always repeats that finesse. No shaking or quivering when you duck with the queen.

400* Sometimes the number of tricks declarer has available can be inferred by the way declarer tackles the suit.

(a) **North** (dummy)
A1054

West (you)
K3

East
J987

South
Q62

If declarer leads low to the queen, partner playing the nine, (count), play declarer for one trick in the suit. Partner clearly has the jack. Had declarer both the queen and the jack, she would have started with an honor from the closed hand.

(b) **North** (dummy)
AJ65

West (you)
K92

East
10873

South
Q4

If declarer leads low to the queen (partner giving count), play declarer for two tricks in the suit. If declarer had the ten or Qxxx, declarer would have started the suit from her own hand.

401* When partner shows out of a suit, meaning declarer knows your EXACT holding, give partner the same information. WHATEVER DECLARER KNOWS, PARTNER MUST ALSO BE TOLD.

North (dummy)
32

West
5

East (you)
109874

South
AKQJ6

Say South bangs down the AK. Your first play, the four, is count; your second, the ten, shows your highest remaining equal.

402* Attacking a "last hope" suit with a small card when RHO has weakness PROMISES the ace or king. With 10xx(x), Jxx(x) or Qxx(x), attack with the honor.
With two unequal honors and THREE card length, attack with the lower honor. Lead the jack from AJx or KJx; the ten from A10x, K10x or Q10x.
With A9x, K9x or Q9x, attack with the nine in order to unblock the suit. (See tip 398, second example)

North (dummy)
82

West
AQ73

East (you)
K95

South
J1064

If this is a "last hope" suit, attack with the nine.

MISCELLANEOUS

403* When the bidding tells you that partner has a stray queen, king, or ace, assume it is one you need.

Neither side vul.
Dealer East

North (dummy)
♠ 632
♥ Q109
♦ A1095
♣ QJ9

East (you)
♠ K9875
♥ AJ76
♦ K42
♣ 8

East	**South**	**West**	**North**
1♠	1NT	Pass	3NT
All Pass			

Opening lead: ♠10

South wins the opening lead with the jack and runs the ♦J to your king, partner playing the ♦3. Now what?

A few preliminaries: (1) The lead tells you that declarer has three spade tricks: (2) looking at 20 HCP between your hand and dummy and assigning declarer an average 17, your only chance is that partner is looking at a king. As the ♣K is not enough, assume it is the ♥K and shift to a low heart before declarer runs away and hides with 10 tricks.

Declarer's hand: ♠ AQJ ♥ 832 ♦ QJ7 ♣ AK105
Partner's hand: ♠ 104 ♥ K54 ♦ 863 ♣ 76432

(11)
COUNTING DECLARER'S TRICKS AND DUMMY RECOGNITION (SUIT)

Counting declarer's tricks at a suit contract is linked to the trump suit. The defending side must be alive to the likely number of trump tricks available in the combined hands.

When the declaring side has eight or more trump, the norm, declarer's plan may include ruffing in the short hand, crossruffing, long suit establishment, or developing an endplay. In many cases the defense has a counter to each of these attacks. The crux to most defensive strategies (and trick counting) lies in recognizing the type of dummy that appears and having the right answer to each one.

TYPE I DUMMY- BALANCED

404* The best defense against a balanced hand is usually PASSIVE. Avoid breaking new suits, give declarer what she is entitled to; sit back and wait for your tricks. Unless either declarer or dummy has a side four card suit that can be set up for a discard, DECLARER'S LOSERS WILL NOT VANISH. (If it is declarer who has the side four card suit, the discard from dummy will only be helpful if trumps can be drawn and dummy still remains with at least one trump). If declarer is playing a 5-3 trump fit, this worry is minimal.

East- West vul.
Dealer South

North (dummy)
♠ 643
♥ K106
♦ AJ10
♣ J632

West (you)
♠ AKJ
♥ 983
♦ 975
♣ K1086

South	**West**	**North**	**East**
1♥	Pass	2♥	All Pass

Opening lead: ♠A
Partner plays the ♠2, declarer the ♠8, plan your defense.

Three thoughts should register:
(1) Dummy is balanced (type I).
(2) Dummy's fourth club does not look dangerous.
(3) Partner's play of the ♠2 is ATTITUDE: not count, and not suit preference. All signs indicate a passive defense; shift to a trump at trick two and let declarer find her own way.

Declarer's hand: ♠ Q98 ♥ AQ742 ♦ K43 ♣ Q5
Partner's hand: ♠ 10752 ♥ J5 ♦ Q862 ♣ A97

Declarer can still prevail with a trump lead, but may not. Any other return is just too friendly.

TYPE II DUMMY-A LONG SUIT AND A SHORT SUIT(S)

405. When dummy comes down with both a long and a short suit, (TYPE II), your strategy depends upon the danger of the long suit. If it appears establishable (or already established) ATTACK! If you know that the long suit is harmless, best defense is usually to lead a trump to cut down dummy's ruffing power. DECLARER'S SIDE SUIT LOSERS CANNOT GET AWAY.

Both sides vul.
Dealer South

North (dummy)
♠ Q95
♥ A108765
♦ 32
♣ 32

West (you)
♠ A43
♥ 4
♦ Q1084
♣ KJ654

South	West	North	East
1♠	Pass	2♠	Pass
4♠	All Pass		

Opening lead: ♥4

Dummy plays the ♥A, and declarer the ♥Q. At trick two declarer leads a low diamond to the nine and your ten, partner playing the ♦5. Now what?

A type II has hit the table. When declarer rises with the ♥A, and leads a diamond to the nine and ten, it is clear that the hearts are harmless and the best defense is ace and a trump.

Declarer's hand: ♠ KJ10876 ♥ Q ♦ AJ96 ♣ A10
Partner's hand: ♠ 2 ♥ KJ932 ♦ K75 ♣ Q987

Reduced to but one ruff in dummy, declarer can come to only nine tricks: five spades in the closed hand, one diamond ruff in dummy and three side aces.

406* At times only one of the defenders will know whether dummy's length is dangerous or not. If that defender adapts a passive defense, the other defender must assume that the long suit is under control and defend accordingly.

Neither side vul.
Dealer North

North (dummy)
♠ AKQ4
♥ 42
♦ AKJ9
♣ 1043

West
♠ 65
♥ QJ98
♦ 543
♣ AJ92

East (you)
♠92
♥ A1053
♦ Q1087
♣ Q85

South
♠ J10873
♥ K76
♦ 62
♣ K76

North	East	South	West
1♦	Pass	1♠	Pass
4♠	All Pass		

Opening lead: ♥Q

When dummy hits, you know that it is a type I dummy because YOU have the diamonds bottled up. If you win the ♥A and return a heart instead of a club, partner will know as much as well. With diamond weakness, you would have shifted to a club.

TYPE III DUMMY- A LONG, POWERFUL, SIDE SUIT

407. When dummy hits with a powerful side suit (TYPE III), the defenders must hurry, hurry, hurry, to cash side suit winners. Take care, however: some suits must be attacked by a particular defender.

Both sides vul.
Dealer **South**

North (dummy)
♠ A32
♥ 2
♦ AKQ109
♣ 7652

East (you)
♠ 9
♥ AJ943
♦ 8765
♣ Q98

South	West	North	East
3♠	Pass	4♠	All Pass

Opening lead: ♥K (Plan your defense)

Clearly a TYPE III dummy. Overtake the opening lead and shift to the ♣Q. You need THREE quick club tricks so you must play partner for the AJ10. Had the contract been 5♠, you would still overtake, but you would shift to a LOW club to give declarer a guess in case she had KJ(x).

Declarer's hand: ♠ KQJ10876 ♥ 765 ♦ - ♣ K43
Partner's hand: ♠ 54 ♥ KQ108 ♦ J432 ♣ AJ10

408* When a Type III dummy hits, do not panic. Simply try to place the MINIMUM honor strength necessary in partner's hand to defeat the contract and defend accordingly.

Both sides vul.
Dealer **West**

North (dummy)
♠ 7
♥ AJ84
♦ 853
♣ AQJ103

West (you)
♠ AK8
♥ 72
♦ A1042
♣ 9752

West	**North**	**East**	**South**
1♦	2♣	Pass	2♥
Pass	4♥	All Pass	

Opening lead: ♠A

Partner plays the ♠2. What do you play at trick two?

In order to defeat this contract you must find partner with strong diamonds or any diamond honor plus the ♣K. Shift to a low diamond to cater to either possibility. If you shifted to a club because:

(1) The ♠2 showed club strength; it didn't.
(2) Leading through strength is clever; it isn't. Leading through SHORT suit strength is fine, leading through long suit strength is dangerous. Sometimes declarer has the missing honor! And even if partner has the missing honor, it may be too late to establish tricks in another suit once dummy's long suit is established.

Declarer's hand: ♠ Q103 ♥ KQ1065 ♦ KQ9 ♣ 86
Partner's hand: ♠ J96542 ♥ 93 ♦ J76 ♣ K4

409* When dummy tables with a solid suit (clearly TYPE III), and declarer is known to have a singleton in that suit, leading that suit BEFORE declarer can draw trump may put that suit to rest. It now becomes a question of whether trumps can drawn and the side suit still used.

Neither side vul.
Dealer South

North (dummy)
♠ QJ6
♥ AKQJ3
♦ 932
♣ 74

West (you)
♠ 9432
♥ 97
♦ KJ8
♣ K1083

East
♠ 8
♥ 106542
♦ 105
♣ A9652

South
♠ AK1075
♥ 8
♦ AQ764
♣ QJ

South	West	North	East
1♠	Pass	2♥	Pass
3♦	Pass	4♠	All Pass

Opening lead: ♣3

Partner wins and returns a club to your king. The bidding marks declarer with all the missing honors so the only hope is to kill the heart suit in order to score later diamond tricks. If you shift to a heart at trick three, declarer will win and play a high and low trump to dummy hoping to draw trump ending in dummy. When that doesn't pan out, declarer can no longer make the hand.

410*

410* When a potentially dangerous side suit is lurking in dummy, (suit A), and declarer is EVENTUALLY going to discard a loser or losers (in suit B), attack suit B.

Neither side vul.
Dealer West

North (dummy)
♠ A985
♥ 4
♦ KJ93
♣ 8653

East (you)
♠ J73
♥ AJ862
♦ 8742
♣ 7

West	North	East	South
2♦*	Pass	4♥	5♣
All Pass.			

* Flannery- five hearts, four spades 11-16 HCP.

Opening lead: ♥K (Plan your defense)

Declarer is known to hold two spades and two hearts and six or seven clubs. Whatever, the second spade (suit B) is going to be discarded on the diamonds (suit A) sooner or later. Overtake the lead and switch to a spade playing partner for either a diamond or a trump entry.

Declarer's hand: ♠Q2 ♥ 53 ♦ AQ10 ♣ AQJ1092
Partner's hand: ♠K1064 ♥ KQ1097 ♦ 65 ♣ K4

411* If urgency is key (Type III), and partner needs one of two specific cards to defeat the contract, the idea is not to guess. There may be another way.

East-West vul.
Dealer South

North (dummy)
♠ 84
♥ J7
♦ KJ106
♣ AKJ105

East (you)
♠ AJ73
♥ A954
♦ 52
♣ 876

South	West	North	East
1♦	Pass	2♣	Pass
2♦	Pass	4♦	Pass
5♦	All Pass		

Opening lead: ♥3. You win the ace and declarer plays the eight. Now what?

If partner has either major suit king, the contract is doomed. Rather than guess, play the ♠A at trick two. If partner encourages, continue with a spade; if partner discourages, revert to hearts.

412* If declarer's reentry to an established suit is in the trump suit, forcing the dummy to ruff could put this suit to sleep.

Both sides vul.
Dealer South

North (dummy)
♠ K4
♥ 98
♦ A95
♣ AK8743

West (you)
♠ QJ97
♥ K63
♦ 732
♣ Q109

East
♠ A632
♥ Q10754
♦ 6
♣ J52

South
♠ 1085
♥ AJ2
♦ KQJ1084
♣ 6

South winds up in 5♦ (bring back 3NT) and you lead the ♠Q. Partner tops the king and returns the ♠2 showing four. Your play is to win and play a third spade forcing dummy to ruff. Declarer can no longer establish clubs AND draw trump ending in dummy. You have killed the club suit and your reward is the setting trick in hearts.

413* If the entry to what will soon be an established side suit can be removed early, the side suit is dead meat.

Both sides vul.
Dealer West

North (dummy)
♠ 10862
♥ 3
♦ KQ
♣ KQJ1094

West (you)
♠ AK543
♥ 76
♦ A1052
♣ 32

East
♠ QJ9
♥ 1054
♦ 764
♣ A876

South
♠ 7
♥ AKQJ982
♦ J983
♣ 5

West	North	East	South
1♠	2♣	2♠	4♥
All Pass			

Opening lead: ♠K (K from AK after the suit has been supported)

The bidding indicates that declarer has strong hearts leaving partner with a likely ♣A. In order to kill the EVENTUAL entry to the clubs, switch to a LOW diamond and retain control. Declarer does best to play a club, but if partner wins and returns a trump (or a diamond to your ace followed by a trump), the contract is defeated. Partner should realize that you are not the one with the singleton club because you neither led nor shifted to a club. (see tip 372)

414* When the defense cannot afford to give up the lead, Type III dummies often present interesting cash out problems. Watching count signals suddenly becomes a matter of life and death.

East-West vul.
Dealer South

North (dummy)
♠ J43
♥ AQ5
♦ J6
♣ AKQ108

East (you)
♠ AKQ
♥ 106
♦ A974
♣ 9743

South	**West**	**North**	**East**
3♥	Pass	4♥	All Pass

Opening lead: ♠10

You win the opening lead with the queen and cash a second spade, partner playing the nine, declarer following. What next?

Clearly you must try to cash FOUR tricks between spades and diamonds. In order to know how many diamond tricks you need, you must know how many spade tricks your side has coming. Enter the present count signal. Partner's play of the ♠9, present count, indicates an original holding of three or five spades. As five spades seems more likely, declarer has no more spades and your side needs two diamond tricks. Shift to a low diamond and give declarer a guess if she has the king. Had partner shown four spades (by playing her lowest), you would know to cash a third spade and then the ♦A.

It is important that you learn how to give and receive present count signals. (See tip 159)

Declarer's hand: ♠ 65 ♥ KJ98742 ♦ K10 ♣ 52
Partner's ♠ 109872 ♥ 3 ♦ Q8532 ♣ J6

AVOIDING ACCIDENTS — BUILDING FENCES — (PARTNER'S ERRORS)

415* TYPE III dummies lend themselves to "accidents". The definition of an accident is partner making a mistake that you could have avoided. A sure-fire way to avoid an accident is not to give partner a chance to make any decisions.

Both sides vul.
Dealer East

North (dummy)
♠ AQJ1082
♥ 75
♦ KJ108
♣ Q

West (you)
♠ 9
♥ K98
♦ 2
♣ AK1098632

East	**South**	**West**	**North**
Pass	1♦	4♣	4♠
5♣	Pass	Pass	5♦
All Pass			

Opening lead: ♣K

Partner plays the ♣4, declarer follows.
Plan a non-accident prone defense.

It looks like the best chance to defeat the contract is to find partner with either the ♥A or the ♥Q and the ♠K. In either case it is right to shift to a heart. In order to avoid an accident, shift to the ♥K. What accident? Leading a low heart, finding partner with the ace, and having partner return a spade hoping you can ruff because she thought your ♥8 lead was top of nothing. Leave no prisoners, take charge.

Declarer's hand: ♠K ♥ QJ32 ♦ AQ96543 ♣ 7
Partner's hand: ♠ 76543 ♥ A1064 ♦ 7 ♣ J54

East-West vul.
Dealer South

North (dummy)
♠ 62
♥ AJ65
♦ J32
♣ KJ102

East (you)
♠ 109
♥ Q109
♦ A1074
♣ Q943

South	**West**	**North**	**East**
1♠	Pass	1NT	Pass
2♥	Pass	3♥	All Pass

Opening lead: ♦K

Partner continues with the queen and a diamond to your ace, declarer following. What now?

Although everyone on the planet knows that declarer has a singleton club, your partner may be the lone exception. Lead a low club before declarer does. Now partner can't make a mistake.

Declarer's hand: ♠ AKQ74 ♥ K874 ♦ 985 ♣ 5
Partner's hand: ♠ J853 ♥ 32 ♦ KQ6 ♣ A876

KEEP COUNTING!

416* There will be times where you won't be able to prevent declarer from establishing dummy's long suit. However, even if the suit is established and used, the hand may still not be over. Count tricks!

Both sides vul.
Dealer North

North (dummy)
♠ A75
♥ KQ87
♦ AJ1043
♣ 10

West
♠ 10982
♥ 3
♦ 865
♣ Q9732

East (you)
♠ KQ6
♥ 942
♦ Q92
♣ A854

South
♠ J43
♥ AJ1065
♦ K7
♣ KJ6

North	East	South	West
1♦	Pass	1♥	Pass
3♥	Pass	4♦	Pass
6♥	All Pass		

Opening lead: ♠10

Declarer wins the ♠A, establishes the diamonds with one ruff and draws three rounds of trump ending in dummy. Are you counting tricks? Declarer has six trump tricks (five in her own hand plus an eventual club ruff in dummy) to go along with four diamonds and the ♠A for a grand total of 11. You are still alive! Somehow you must get TWO club tricks. After declarer discards two spades on the diamonds and leads a club, DUCK. If declarer has ♣KJx and misguesses, the contract is defeated.

417* You know you have "arrived" when you can determine whether tricks can vanish in a particular suit if not attacked quickly, or if those tricks cannot get away if the suit is left untouched. The answer lies in counting declarer's tricks in the other suits.

Both sides vul.
Dealer South

North (dummy)
♠ AQ7
♥ AKQ10
♦ J654
♣ J7

East (you)
♠ 6
♥ (1) J9432 or (2) 95432
♦ Q103
♣ AK104

South	West	North	East
2♠	Pass	4♠	All Pass

Opening lead: ♣3

You win the first two club tricks, partner showing a five card suit. What should you lead at trick three? Count declarer's tricks before you answer. Declarer has six spade winners and depending upon your heart holding three or four heart tricks. Clearly, partner needs the ♦A to defeat the contract; and equally clear from the non-diamond lead is that declarer has the ♦K.

With (1) there is no need to attack diamonds, as declarer has only nine tricks and will have to attack diamonds herself losing two tricks in the suit. However with (2), because of the fortuitous heart lie, declarer has ten tricks; six spades and four hearts. Diamonds must be attacked at once; shift to a low diamond at trick three and hope declarer misguesses. With (1), shift to a trump at trick three and sit back and wait for your two diamond tricks. So, have you arrived?

Declarer's hand: ♠ KJ10832 ♥ 76 ♦ K87 ♣ 86
Partner's hand: ♠ 954 ♥ 85 or J8 ♦ A92 ♣ Q9532

Neither side vul.
Dealer North

North (dummy)
♠ K43
♥ K10
♦ Q76
♣ KQ972

East (you)
♠ A10
♥ AQ4
♦ K982
♣ 10654

North	**East**	**South**	**West**
1♣	Pass	1♥	Pass
1NT	Pass	3♥	All Pass

Opening lead: ♣3

Another "arrival" hand. Declarer wins the opening lead with the ace and leads a heart to the king and ace. You return a low club which partner ruffs with the ♥9. Partner exits with the ♦J which is covered by the queen, king and ace. When declarer leads a second heart to dummy's ten, partner discards the ♠9. What is your "arrival" play?

Declarer is known to have six hearts and three clubs along with four other cards. Judging from partner's violent spade discard, partner has at least the queen to go along with the ♦10. So what can go wrong? Everything! You must return a CLUB and let declarer discard ONE loser on the fourth club. You will ruff the fifth club and no matter what declarer's two remaining cards are, your side takes two more tricks.

Declarer's hand: ♠ J65 ♥ J87632 ♦ A ♣ AJ8
Partner's hand: ♠ Q9872 ♥ 95 ♦ J10543 ♣ 3

If you return a "safe" diamond, declarer ruffs, draws your last trump and discards two spades on the fourth and fifth club. (For a similar defensive conception—killing dummy's length while you still have a trump — see tip 409).

COUNTING THEIR TRUMP TRICKS

418* When counting declarer's trump tricks, be sure to include ruffs in the SHORT hand.

(a)

North (dummy)
AJ65

West
82

East
943

South
KQ107

If declarer draws three rounds of trump, count declarer for five trump tricks as declarer can almost always use the two remaining trump separately. If declarer is crossruffing, there is a possibility of eight trump tricks. However, each time a trump is led, the trick count in the trump suit is reduced by one.

(b)

North (dummy)
AQ7

South
KJ10832

Assume declarer is marked with a strong six card suit. Count declarer for six trump tricks PLUS any short suit ruffs available. For example, if dummy has a doubleton and declarer has three cards in that suit, it is likely that declarer can get a seventh trump trick by ruffing once in dummy.

(c)

North (dummy)
8632

West (you)
Q105

East
J9

South
AK74

Say declarer plays the AK of trump leaving you with the queen. If declarer can trump two cards in dummy and two cards in her hand without you overtrumping, she can take SIX trump tricks. Now consider this scenario: Declarer plays the AK of trump and lets you in in a side suit. If you cash the high trump, you limit declarer to a maximum of FOUR trump tricks. A word to the wise.

(d)

North (dummy)
KJ93

West (you)
A62

East
75

South
Q1084

If you lead a low trump and (before any ruffing starts), you get in and lead the ace and a trump, the opponents can get no more than four trump tricks.

419. If dummy has a short suit and declarer does not go for even one short suit ruff, assume declarer has no losers in that suit and do not count any short suit ruffs. (See tip #296)

(12)
DECEPTIVE PLAYS

Deceptive plays are meant to fool the declarer, not partner. They are made for the purpose of giving declarer a false impression of what really exists. The trick is to visualize the holding you want declarer to IMAGINE you have, and then play your cards as if you had that holding. (Help!)

Do not false card without a reason. Playing higher cards than necessary or winning tricks with the higher of two or three equals or returning the wrong card can all be misleading and cause partner to miscount and later misdefend. The idea is to familiarize yourself with the common deceptive plays and be ready to use them without giving away the show by hesitating. The majority of deceptive plays are made in suits that the declarer attacks as opposed to suits either you or your partner are leading.

BASICS

420* If it cannot cost a trick, PLAY THE CARD OR CARDS YOU ARE KNOWN TO HOLD AS SOON AS POSSIBLE. A BIGGIE.

(a)

	North (dummy) A832	
West K54		**East** (you) J97
	South Q106	

After declarer leads low to the ten and king, your jack and nine are EQUALS and declarer KNOWS you have the JACK, but doesn't know you have the nine. The next time the suit is played, play the JACK the card you are known to hold. If declarer believes you, she will lead low to the eight after cashing the queen. If you insist upon clutching your jack, you have zero chance of taking a trick with a card that has become an albatross.

(b)

	North (dummy) A7652	
West (you) (1) QJ104 (2) KQJ		**East** K83 10843
	South 9	

The suit you see is hearts and spades are trump. After you lead the queen with (1) and the king with (2), declarer wins and sooner or later ruffs a heart. With (1) play the jack, the card you are known to hold from the lead; with (2) play the queen for the same reason. As long as you keep the cards you are known to hold, declarer can ruff hearts back to her hand with low trump.

(c) **North** (dummy)
AQ75

West (you)
KJ93

East
1064

South
82

South leads low to the queen, cashes the ace and then ruffs the suit back to her hand. Not so fast. Under the ace drop the king the card you are known to hold. Now declarer will think twice before ruffing this suit with a low trump—you may overtrump.

(d) **North** (dummy)
KJ

West (you)
AQ42

East
876

South
10953

This is a side suit in a trump contract. Early in the hand declarer leads low to the king which wins. When the jack is continued, win the trick with the ACE, the card you are known to hold. (The ace and queen are equals so you are not "wasting" anything, just trying to mislead declarer).

(e) **North** (dummy)
A10864

West
93

East (you)
KJ75

South
Q2

At notrump North leads low to the queen which holds. When South continues by leading low to the ten, win with the king, the card you are known to hold: (Again, the king and jack are equals so you are not wasting anything). Later when declarer plays the ace and you follow low, declarer cannot be sure if the suit is breaking and may make the wrong discard. Winning the ten with the jack gives the whole show away when you later follow with a low card under ace.

LEADS AND RETURNS

421* When partner's lead marks you with a specific honor, and that honor is expendable, get it out of your hand pronto!

North (dummy)
62

West
J1087

East (you)
Q54

South
AK93

Versus a suit contract, partner leads the jack. When declarer plays the ace and then the king with the intention of trumping both losers in dummy, play the queen. Declarer may ruff the third round higher than necessary.

422* When partner's lead can be ambiguous from DECLARER'S point of view, don't be the friendly type that helps declarer out by playing any card that removes the ambiguity.

(a)

North (dummy)
K75

West
J3

East (you)
AQ10864

South
92

Partner leads the jack which is covered by the king and ace. After you cash the queen, continue with the eight, NOT the ten. Do not show declarer that ten, a card partner may have from the lead. Also, if declarer ducks the opening lead, do not signal with the ten, a "friendly" signal if there ever was one.

(b)

North (dummy)
763

West
1062

East (you)
AKQJ54

South
9

When partner leads a supported suit and declarer will either ruff the opening lead or the second round, play the ace and then the queen from an AKQ combination. Declarer is likely to place partner with the king and given that misconception, may misplace other honors.

423* When your lead can be ambiguous from declarer's point of view, but not partner's, try not to clarify the ambiguity.

North (dummy)
A65

West (you)
QJ2

East
K10743

South
98

You hold the lead with the queen in partner's UNSUPPORTED suit. Continue with the deuce, not the jack. Partner knows you have the jack. Had declarer Jxx, the ace would have been played at trick one.

424* When declarer's length is known, and you have a card that will clarify partner's length to declarer, hide that card for all eternity.

North (dummy)
54

West
K1073

East (you)
QJ62

South
A98

Vs. notrump, declarer having denied four cards in this suit, allows your jack to hold the first trick. It is not necessary to return the deuce and tell declarer the suit is breaking 4-4. Return the six. Partner knows you have the queen and knows you have at least four cards in the suit.

425* Versus a suit contract, it is usually safe to underlead a strong holding when dummy is known to be long and strong and declarer is known to be short.

North (dummy)
AJ983

West (you)
KQ7542

East
6

South
10

If dummy has bid this suit, lead low, not the king. Declarer is not looking into your hand and is unlikely to take any Disneyland finesses.

PROTECTING A FINESSABLE TRUMP HONOR

426* When holding a trump honor that can be finessed, try to give the declarer the impression that you have a side suit void. The fear of an impending ruff may dissuade declarer from taking the trump finesse.

	North (dummy) AKQ2	
West 10985		**East** (you) J6
	South 743	

When partner leads the ten, play the jack, a card you are known to hold. If declarer believes you, she may not take the winning trump finesse lest partner win and give you a ruff. Another tactic to steer declarer away from a winning trump finesse is to make a shift smack into dummy's strong suit feigning a singleton (are you tricky, or what?). If declarer believes you, she may be afraid to take the trump finesse. It goes without saying you have to know what you are doing when you try a play like this.

WHEN YOU HOLD ALL OF THE CARDS

427. When KNOWN to be holding a strong hand, use your higher, rather than your lower, equal(s) to win tricks.

	North (dummy) AJ107	
West 9652		**East** (you) KQ
	South 843	

When declarer leads low to the jack, play the king. If you win with the queen and the bidding has marked you with the king, what do you think is going to happen the next time the suit is played?

WHEN GOOD THINGS ARE ABOUT TO HAPPEN

428. When declarer unwittingly attacks your strongest suit, you have several deceptive ploys at your disposal:

(1) Taking the trick with a higher card than necessary to make declarer think things are going well.

(2) Ducking the trick altogether encouraging declarer to lead the suit again in which case the roof will cave in.

(a)

	North (dummy) Q1098	
West 763		**East** (you) AKJ
	South 542	

If declarer leads low to the eight, win the trick with the king. This will encourage declarer to waste a hand entry to lead the suit again... to no avail.

(b)

	North (dummy) Q1098	
West 2		**East** (you) AKJ54
	South 763	

At notrump holding no outside entry, you see declarer lead low to the eight. You might try ducking. If declarer leads the suit again, you can cash four winners.

(c)

	North (dummy) KJ10	
West 2		**East** (you) AQ963
	South 8754	

At notrump declarer leads low to the ten. With no outside entry, it is not a bad idea to play low. Declarer is apt to reenter her hand and lead the suit again. This time you can scoop up four tricks.

429* Another ploy with the AQx(x) sitting over a KJ10(x)(x), combination is to win the ACE when declarer leads low to the ten. This will induce declarer to think that partner has the queen and may dissuade declarer from taking another finesse that really does work. How sneaky.

East-West vul.
Dealer South

North (dummy)
♠ 63
♥ QJ10
♦ KJ1098
♣ AQ9

West
♠ QJ98
♥ 6432
♦ 32
♣ 864

East (you)
♠ 107542
♥ K5
♦ AQ7
♣ 10532

South
♠ AK
♥ A987
♦ 654
♣ KJ7

South	**West**	**North**	**East**
1NT	Pass	3NT	All Pass

Opening lead: ♠Q

Since you can see 22 HCP between your hand and dummy, you know partner's only honors are in spades. Declarer wins and plays a diamond to the jack. If you win the ACE and return a spade, which finesse do you think declarer will take next, diamonds or hearts? If you win the first diamond with the QUEEN and return a spade, which suit do you think declarer is going to attack next, diamonds or hearts? Hint: it won't be diamonds.

CONVERSATIONAL DECEPTIVE PLAYS

430* Put the following deceptive play in your memory bank. If it comes up, you will have a good story to tell for years.

North (dummy)
A10863

West
Q54

East (you)
K9

South
J72

Assume declarer leads the jack and partner covers. When the ace is played, drop the king! Declarer will assume partner has the guarded nine, and will do headstands trying to get back to her hand to run the seven. She may waste a valuable hand entry to do it.

North (dummy)
♣ AQ

West (you)
♣ K4

East
♣ 1072

South
♣ J98653

Assume this is the trump suit and declarer leads low towards dummy. If you play the king and declarer believes you, declarer may try to develop a trump coup against partner's expected 10xxx. This coup may require that declarer does not play a second round of trump. Every so often a defender can ruff a winner as declarer prepares for her non-existent coup. Play the same with Qx when dummy has AK blank. (These plays presume that declarer does not need to ruff a loser in dummy).

MANDATORY FALSE CARDS (AND SWINDLES)

431* When you can diagnose a 4-3 adverse division, and the opponents have the three top honors, playing the jack from Jxx or the jack-ten from J10x can cause unforeseen complications.

(a)

	North (dummy) AK42	
West 876		**East** (you) J93
	South Q105	

If declarer plays queen and low to the king or king and low to the queen, drop the jack on the SECOND round. This has a disconcerting effect upon a strong declarer who thinks the suit is blocked. Good things usually happen.

(b)

	North (dummy) AKQ3	
West 652		**East** (you) J108
	South 974	

Play the jack and the ten under the ace-king. Declarer will probably return to the nine and then may not have a sure dummy entry to cash the fourth round winner. If you do not play your two honors, declarer has no choice but to cash the queen.

432* A good defender is always looking for ways to create finesse positions for declarer where none exist.

(a) **North** (dummy)
K4

West (you) J105 | **East** 86

South
AQ9732

When dummy leads the king or low towards the king, play the ten or jack. Suddenly declarer has the option of leading low to the nine.

(b) **North** (dummy)
K105

West (you) Q4 | **East** J3

South
A98762

This is an insulting suggestion but it has been known to work against very weak players. When South leads the ace, drop the queen. There are a small number of South players who will play low to the ten next. Nothing ventured, nothing gained.

433* When you know that declarer's percentage play is going to work, you may be able to alter those percentages by playing just the right false card.

(a)

North (dummy)
K10876

West
QJ54

East (you)
93

South
A2

South, looking for four tricks at notrump (one side entry) begins with the ace. If you play low, South has no choice but to lead to the ten next. However, if you drop the nine trying to look like like someone with J9 or Q9 doubleton, declarer may lead low to the king.

(b)

North (dummy)
KJ832

West
Q75

East (you)
1094

South
A6

Vs. notrump South leads the ace. Play the nine or ten trying to look like someone with Q9, Q10 or 109 doubleton. If South believes, South will lead low to the king.

(c)

North (dummy)
-

West (you)
10965

East
Q74

South
AKJ832

At suit or notrump South cashes the ace and king. If you play low both times, South has no choice but to play low on the third round hoping someone has Qxx. However, if you play low-nine, declarer has an option. If declarer thinks you have 109x, declarer will continue with the jack in the hopes of blotting out your ten. Ha, ha.

(d) North (dummy)
A1098

West (you)
KJ43

East
62

South
Q75

At notrump (or suit), assume the lead is in dummy and the ten ducked into your hand. Take the trick with the KING!
If partner has the queen, it won't matter. However, if declarer has a likely Qxx, you save a trick.

If you win with the jack, declarer will later run the queen and take three tricks. If you win the ten with the king, no way declarer is going to play you for the jack.

434* Don't discourage declarer from making the percentage play if the percentage play is going to lose.

(a) **North** (dummy)
K108

West
A74

East (you)
QJ92

South
653

The best play with this combination for one trick is to lead low to the eight. If the eight loses to the nine, lead low to the king next. If the eight loses to the jack or queen, lead low to the ten next. Knowing that, you should NOT win the eight with the nine. You should take the trick with a higher honor so declarer can continue by leading low to the ten next.

435* When you have J10x and partner Ax, your job is to make declarer think you have J10 and partner Axx. What you have to do is play an honor the first time the suit is led when you are FOURTH to play.

North (dummy)
52

West (you)
J104

East
A3

South
KQ9876

When South leads low to the king, play the ten or jack. If there are no side entries to dummy, South must guess whether the ace is doubleton (actual case), and exit with a low card, or the J10 is doubleton and exit with the queen. Had you played low originally, South would have no choice but to exit with a low card and play for Ax.

436* Playing second hand high in the face of a strong suit that has NO SIDE SUIT ENTRY can produce some amazing results.

(a) **North** (dummy)
AQJ765

West (you)
K4

East
1093

South
82

When South leads low, play the king! If declarer thinks you have a singleton, declarer will duck. The play also works when you have Kxx and declarer has a DOUBLETON. If you play the king from Kxx and declarer has a singleton, take the first train out of town and leave this book behind.

(b) **North** (dummy)
AKJ652

West (you)
Q10, Q109

East
987, 87

South
43

If South is marked with a doubleton, play the Q. If declarer thinks you have a singleton, she may duck. If declarer turns up with three cards and you play the queen, hop on the same train that the player from the previous example is on. Misery loves company.

437* Second hand "middle" from AJ9 when dummy to your right has 10xx(x) can produce some nifty swindles.

(a)

North (dummy)
10432

West
K

East (you)
AJ9

South
Q8765

When dummy leads low, play the jack. Declarer should be mesmerized into playing the queen. If you play the nine, declarer has more reason to play low.

(b)

North (dummy)
1084

West
765

East (you)
AJ9

South
KQ73

Here the play of the jack might convince declarer that you started with a singleton jack or AJ doubleton. In either case declarer, looking for three tricks, may lead low to the eight.

438. Second hand middle with A108 also has a good chance of scoring an extra trick if LHO has QJxx or KJxx.

(c)

North (dummy)
QJ32

West (you)
A108

East
K54

South
976

Try the ten when declarer leads low. Declarer is apt to lead low to the seven next playing you for a singleton or A10 blank.

439* Playing the jack from J9(x) has a great chance of making an extra trick if dummy to your right leads low from A8x, K8x or Q8x towards a known FOUR card suit.

North (dummy)
A82

West
K73

East (you)
J94

South
Q1065

When dummy leads low, play the jack and don't be too surprised if you take a later trick with the nine.

440* When partner's lead catches you with AKx(x), there are two positions where winning with the ACE and returning a low card may perpetrate a swindle.

(a)

North (dummy)
854

West
J962

East (you)
AK3

South
Q107

Versus suit, partner leads a fourth best deuce, marking declarer with at least three cards. The best shot for three tricks is to win the ACE and return the three.

(b)

North (dummy)
75

West
J932

East (you)
AK64

South
Q108

Versus notrump, a similar swindle is available when you have four cards, partner has four cards, and dummy a doubleton; win the ace and return the four.

441* When declarer has a void and you hold two cards higher than anything dummy has, leading a lower card through declarer is not as dangerous as it appears. Declarer usually trumps leaving both you and partner with safe exit cards later.

North (dummy)
10832

West
9654

East (you)
AQJ7

South
K

If partner leads LOW, winning the ace and returning low should be safe. If you return an honor, neither you nor your partner can safely lead the suit later. If declarer discards a loser on the seven, I can't be reached by fax, mail or phone.

442. Dropping the jack from Jx of trump when partner is also marked with a doubleton honor, may force declarer to take an unnecessary risk to repeat an unnecessary finesse. How's that again?

Both sides vul.
Dealer South

North (dummy)
♠ 10863
♥ 864
♦ AKQ4
♣ 86

West (you)
♠ J5
♥ AKQ
♦ 6
♣ QJ97432

East
♠ K2
♥ 9753
♦ 109532
♣ 105

South
♠ AQ974
♥ J102
♦ J87
♣ AK

South	West	North	East
1♠	2♣	3♠	Pass
4♠	All Pass		

Opening lead: ♥**Q**

You cash three hearts and shift to a high club. Declarer wins, crosses to dummy with a diamond and leads a spade to the queen. Since declarer is marked with five spades, partner must have Kx. If you innocently drop the jack under the queen, declarer will assume partner has Kxx and cross back to a diamond to repeat the finesse. However, this is one crossing that won't work. You will ruff the second round of diamonds with your non-existent trump.

443* Playing the nine (or ten) from 109x to protect partner's doubleton honor is a play that comes up time and time again.

(a)

North
J832

West (you)
1094

East
(1) Q6
(2) K6

South
(1) AK75
(2) AQ75

In (1) if declarer starts by leading either a high honor or towards a high honor, play the nine or ten. If you don't, declarer has no option but to play the other high honor hoping to find someone with Qx. However, if you play the nine, declarer suddenly has alternative plays—like leading the jack trying to smother your presumed 109 doubleton.

In (2) if declarer leads low to the queen, play the nine or ten for the same reason.

444* Playing the nine (or ten) from Q109x when sitting behind AKx(x) works like a charm when partner is short in the suit.

North (dummy)
AK82

West
3

East (you)
Q1095

South
J764

When South leads low to the king, play the nine (or ten). This may induce declarer to return to her hand and lead the jack playing you for a singleton or 109 doubleton.

445* Another very sneaky play is available (usually in the trump suit) when dummy, RHO, has J9x and you have Q10 or K10 doubleton. When dummy leads low, play your higherhonor. Great things can happen.

(a)

North (dummy)
J92

West
763

East (you)
(1) Q10
(2) K10

South
(1) AK854
(2) AQ854

When dummy leads low towards known length and strength, play high. If declarer reads this as a singleton, declarer will win and lead low to the nine. If the length is in dummy and dummy has AK9(x)(x) or AQ9x(x), play second hand high with the Q10 or K10 doubleton.

446* When partner has a singleton and you have a finesseable four card holding, the idea is to make declarer think that you have the singleton and partner has the finessable four card holding. Pretty tricky, huh?

(a)

North (dummy)
KJ92

West (you)
10865

East
A

South
Q743

When declarer leads low towards dummy, play the eight. After partner wins the ace, (or queen), declarer is apt to play you for shortness and continue by playing dummy's remaining honor. If you play low originally, declarer has no choice but to play you for the length.

(b)

North (dummy)
AQ102

West (you)
J976

East
3

South
K854

When South leads low, play the nine. This may induce declarer to think partner has Jxxx and continue with the ace and queen. If you play low, declarer has no option but to play the ace and then low to the king.

Note: In both cases you need strong interior spot cards to make these plays.

447* In order to protect partner's known or suspected blank honor, play any worthless honor you are known to hold the second time the suit is played.

(a)

North(dummy)
AJ9

West
1065

East (you)
KQ

South
87432

South leads low to the nine and queen. The next time South leads low, play the TEN, the card you are known to hold. If you play low and declarer needs all the rest of the tricks, (or has a count), declarer will play the ace knowing that you still have the ten.

(b)

North (dummy)
AQ10873

West (you)
J62

East
K9

South
54

Early on declarer leads low to the ten which holds. When declarer leads the suit again, play the jack, a card she knows you hold. If you don't, and declarer needs the rest of the tricks in this suit (or has a count), partner's king is history.

448* When overruffing dummy with a lower honor will leave your remaining higher honor susceptible to a finesse, overruff with the higher honor to protect the lower honor! Is this tip for real? Yes!

North (dummy)
Q109

West
2

East (you)
KJ64

South
A8753

Assume you have a chance to overtrump dummy's nine. If you over-trump with the jack, your king will soon be finessed and you wind up with one trump trick. If you overtrump with the KING, you are a mortal cinch to win a second trick with the jack, a card declarer thinks your partner has.

449. Vs. suit, leading the queen from an AQJ10(x) combination through a KNOWN king in dummy, usually works. Declarer, thinking your partner has the ace, almost always ducks. However, if declarer unexpectedly turns up with a singleton king or a small singleton and plays the king from dummy, this tip is a misprint.

MISCELLANEOUS

450. Ask yourself what declarer knows about your hand from the bidding and your previous plays. The more she knows, the more susceptible you will be to deceptive plays. In other words, do not play declarer for making any tricky plays unless she knows what you have.

451. If a competent declarer makes a strange looking play from dummy at trick one, careful!

North (dummy)
Q107

West
9

East (you)
AJ43

South
?

Vs. notrump partner leads the nine and dummy plays low. Why is declarer being so good to you and not covering with the ten? Why? Because declarer wants you to duck the trick. Declarer is afraid that if you win the trick you might shift to another weaker suit.

452. Don't expect this to happen very often, but at notrump expert declarers have been known to attack their WEAKEST suit to throw you off the scent. Just be aware that the possibility exists.

(13)
FORGING EXTRA TRICKS IN THE TRUMP SUIT

When defending a suit contract you are usually outgunned pointwise and may have to pick up the slack either by getting a ruff, giving a ruff, preventing declarer from ruffing, or forcing dummy or declarer to ruff. Defenders must always have their antennae poised looking for extra tricks in the trump suit. A good start is knowing partner's trump length. Don't be shy about projecting a trump honor(s) or even a significant trump spot card in partner's hand. WHEN IT IS CLEAR THAT THERE ARE NO TRICKS COMING FROM THE SIDE SUITS, LOOK TO THE TRUMP SUIT.

GIVING PARTNER A RUFF

453* When partner leads an obvious singleton in a suit in which you have two winners, it may be right to give partner a ruff BEFORE cashing the second winner (if cashing the second winner will set up later discards for declarer).

Both sides vul.
Dealer South

North (dummy)
♠ KJ3
♥ QJ109
♦ AQ6
♣ J92

West
♠ 942
♥ 2
♦ 87432
♣ 10873

East (you)
♠ 5
♥ AK876
♦ K95
♣ Q654

South
♠ AQ10876
♥ 543
♦ J10
♣ AK

South	**West**	**North**	**East**
1♠	Pass	2NT	Pass
3♠	Pass	**4♠**	All Pass

Opening lead: **♥2**

Your best chance to defeat the contract is to assume the lead is a singleton. Win the ♥K and return the ♥8, suit preference for diamonds. After partner ruffs and returns a diamond, declarer is helpless. If you cash both hearts first, you don't get a diamond trick.

454* When partner leads a singleton in dummy's most powerful suit and finds you with the ace, and only one ruff is available, it may be necessary to lead a QJ suit through declarer's presumed king first. It all depends upon the number of tricks you need to defeat the contract.

Neither side vul.
Dealer South

North (dummy)
♠ KQJ94
♥ KQ6
♦ AKQ
♣ 87

West
♠ 2
♥ 852
♦ 10832
♣ A9542

East (you)
♠ A8765
♥ 4
♦ J976
♣ QJ6

South
♠ 103
♥ AJ10973
♦ 54
♣ K103

South	**West**	**North**	**East**
2♥	Pass	4♥	All Pass

Opening lead: **♠2**

After winning the ♠A, it is clear that giving partner one ruff is not enough. Your side needs TWO club tricks as well as the ruff. Project the ♣A in partner's hand and switch to the ♣Q. If declarer covers, your ♣J is the reentry for the spade ruff; if declarer ducks the ♣Q, give partner a spade ruff and the ♣A is the setting trick.

455* When giving partner a ruff, give suit preference. With no preference, ask partner to return a "neutral" suit as opposed to one that could cost a trick.

East-West vul.
Dealer North

North (dummy)
♠ 10943
♥ AQJ6
♦ AQ
♣ J76

East (you)
♠ AJ754
♥ K2
♦ 932
♣ 982

North	**East**	**South**	**West**
1♣	Pass	1♥	Pass
2♥	Pass	4♥	All Pass

Opening lead: ♠2

You win the ace and declarer plays the eight. Plan your defense.

As partner is marked with a singleton, return the ♠7 to ask for a diamond return, a return that can't cost; a club return may cost.

Declarer's hand: ♠ KQ8 ♥ 109875 ♦ J104 ♣ AQ
Partner's hand: ♠ 2 ♥ 43 ♦ K8765 ♣ K10543

456* If partner is void in one suit yet makes an encouraging discard in another, partner has "spoken". She does NOT want a ruff. Lead the suit she has requested, it only hurts for a little while.

Neither side vul.
Dealer West

North (dummy)
♠ Q105
♥ 10
♦ AQJ62
♣ KQ84

West
♠ 3
♥ J876
♦ K83
♣ A10973

East (you)
♠ AK98762
♥ 3
♦ 95
♣ 652

South
♠ J4
♥ AKQ9542
♦ 1075
♣ J

West	**North**	**East**	**South**
Pass	1♦	3♠	4♥
All Pass			

Opening lead: ♠3

When you cash a second spade, partner discards an encouraging club. Return a club, not a spade. Had partner wanted a spade, she would have played a discouraging club. If you cross partner's intentions and play a third spade, declarer discards a club while partner ruffs with a natural trump trick. Beautiful, just beautiful.

457* When declarer attacks a side suit and partner unexpectedly ruffs the first round, give suit preference, not count.

North (dummy)
A7

West (you)
Q1086432

East

South
KJ95

Early in the hand declarer goes to ruff losers in this suit and begins with the ace. When partner ruffs, give suit preference.

458. Beware of the fake trump finesse when partner is sitting over there drooling for a ruff.

North (dummy)
K764

West (you)
A5

East
92

South
QJ1083

Declarer, fearing a ruff, leads the jack of trump to make you think she is taking a finesse. If you fall for this, partner loses her ruff.

459. When you hold the ace of a bid and supported suit and partner leads another suit, your suspicions should be aroused. If partner is not leading from an honor sequence, the lead is a likely singleton or doubleton.

460* When partner leads a singleton and you have the ace of trump plus side suit shortness, void yourself BEFORE giving partner a ruff. When you eventually give partner a ruff, she can return the favor.

East-West vul.
Dealer East

North (dummy)
♠ KJ103
♥ AK
♦ Q1076
♣ Q109

West
♠ 642
♥ 10954
♦ A4
♣ 8642

East (you)
♠ A7
♥ J8732
♦ K832
♣ A5

South
♠ Q985
♥ Q6
♦ J95
♣ KJ73

East	**South**	**West**	**North**
1♥	Pass	2♥	Dbl.
Pass	2♠	All Pass	

Opening lead: ♦A

You signal encouragement and partner continues the suit. It is easy enough to give partner a diamond ruff, but that along with your two black aces is only five tricks. A better effort is to swing ace and a club first, grab the first spade and then give partner a diamond ruff. Partner can give you a club ruff in return for down one. If you give partner a diamond ruff prematurely, you remove her entry to give you the club ruff.

461* When partner leads a singleton in dummy's long suit and you have the ace of that suit as well as the ace of trump, but you can only give partner one ruff, try to develop a side suit winner before giving partner her ruff.

Neither side vul.
Dealer South

North (dummy)
♠ J98
♥ 1098
♦ KQJ987
♣ K

West
♠ 62
♥ K432
♦ 2
♣ J65432

East (you)
♠ A43
♥ 765
♦ A65
♣ Q987

South
♠ KQ1075
♥ AQJ
♦ 1043
♣ A10

South	**West**	**North**	**East**
1♠	Pass	2♦	Pass
2NT	Pass	3♠	Pass
4♠	All Pass		

Opening lead: ♦**2**

The bidding tells you partner has two spades, so only one ruff is available. Better to try to establish a heart trick before returning a diamond. Switch to a heart at trick two. If you give partner a diamond ruff, your lose your heart trick on the diamonds.

GOING FOR YOUR OWN RUFF

462* If you hold the ace of trump plus a singleton (and partner needs the ace in your singleton suit to defeat the contract), lead your singleton AFTER you win (or lead) the ace of trump. If you switch to your singleton early, partner may duck playing you for a doubleton (and the ace of trump).

Neither side vul.
Dealer North

North (dummy)
♠ J
♥ QJ106
♦ AK7
♣ KJ864

West
♠ 1072
♥ 43
♦ J9532
♣ A72

East
♠ A98653
♥ A2
♦ Q864
♣ 9

South
♠ KQ4
♥ K9875
♦ 10
♣ Q1053

North	**East**	**South**	**West**
1♣	1♠	2♥	Pass
4♥	All Pass		

Opening lead: **♠2**

When you win the ♠A, it is dangerous to shift to a club because partner may read it as a doubleton and duck. You can make life easier for partner by continuing a spade, (not a diamond), and then shifting to a club upon winning the ♥A. If you shift to a diamond, partner may play you for a singleton diamond when you eventually lead a club! The clearest defense of all is to cash the ♥A at trick two and then shift to a club.

463* If you think you may be leading from unreadable shortness, and you fear partner will win and shift to a more tempting suit in which you have the ace, cash the ace first, denying the king, and then lead your short suit.

North-South vul.
Dealer West

North (dummy)
♠ Q83
♥ 83
♦ K95
♣ AKQJ10

West
♠ 5
♥ KJ10742
♦ Q42
♣ 932

East (you)
♠ K7
♥ AQ
♦ A8763
♣ 8764

South
♠ AJ109642
♥ 965
♦ J10
♣ 5

West	**North**	**East**	**South**
2♥	3♣	3♥	3♠
Pass	4♠	All Pass	

Opening lead: ♥**J** (standard leads)

Your only realistic hope is for partner to overtake your queen of hearts and play a third heart so you can overtrump dummy. The problem is that partner (remember her?) may think it is better to overtake and shift to a diamond in case you have the the ace-jack of diamonds along with THREE hearts. In order to deflect partner from going astray (again), cash the ♦A before returning the ♥Q. With partner's most likely option removed, a third heart will look much more appealing.

464* If you hold the AKx(x)x) in the suit partner has led plus a side suit singleton, win the opening lead with the ACE and then shift to your singleton. Partner, thinking declarer has the king, will be more apt to give you a ruff. If you win the opening lead with the KING and then switch to shortness, partner should assume a doubleton. (With a singleton you would have won the first trick with the ace). Does anybody remember when bridge used to be fun?

Neither side vul.
Dealer East

North (dummy)
♠ 86
♥ KJ86
♦ QJ86
♣ A42

East (you)
♠ AKJ743
♥ 32
♦ 5
♣ QJ98

East	**South**	**West**	**North**
1♠	2♥	3♠*	**4♥**
4♠	5♥	All Pass	

*Preemptive

Opening lead: **♠2**

Plan your defense

Win the ♠A and shift to your diamond. With a diamond winner, partner will be far more inclined to return a diamond than a spade. Remember, partner thinks declarer has the ♠K.

Declarer's hand: ♠ 9 ♥ AQ1094 ♦ K10432 ♣ K3
Partner's hand: ♠ Q1052 ♥ 75 ♦ A97 ♣ 10765

465** Having led from shortness in a suit which the opponents have all of the tricks, giving a high-low in the trump suit shows you have at least one more trump plus being void in the suit you have led.

466* Holding AQ or KQ doubleton and being third to play, win with the higher honor and return the lower honor if you need three quick tricks via a ruff.

North (dummy)
J1064

West (you)
(1) AQ
(2) KQ

East
(1) K852
(2) A852

South
973

If partner leads low (showing a high honor), win the trick with your higher honor and return your lower honor to show a doubleton. An alert partner will overtake and give you a ruff.

467* With a side suit void, it may be necessary to put partner in by leading an unconventional card. The idea is to keep partner focused on giving you a ruff.

East-West vul.
Dealer West

North (dummy)
♠ KJ76
♥ 75
♦ AJ73
♣ AQ9

West (you)
♠ A5
♥ KQJ842
♦ 4
♣ K853

West	**North**	**East**	**South**
1♥	Dbl.	2♥	3♠
4♥	4♠	All Pass	

Opening lead: ♦4

Dummy plays low, partner plays the ♦10 and declarer wins the ♦K. At trick two the ♠10 is led. Plan your defense.

Win the ♠A and switch to the QUEEN of hearts. You don't want partner to duck and you don't want partner to think about returning a heart. The queen is just the right card because it denies the king; partner will be forced to take the ace and look elsewhere for tricks. Maybe "elsewhere" will be that diamond ruff. If it all comes to pass, you can ruff and exit with a heart, eventually taking the setting trick in clubs.

Declarer's hand: ♠ Q10943 ♥ 10 ♦ KQ92 ♣ J74
Partner's hand: ♠82 ♥ A963 ♦ 10865 ♣ 1062

468* When partner's lead indicates an equal honor and you are looking desperately for a later entry to partner's hand to secure a ruff, relax; you have just found it.

North-South vul.
Dealer North

North (dummy)
♠ K4
♥ AJ83
♦ AKQ96
♣ 95

East (you)
♠ A972
♥ Q42
♦ J
♣ AKQ74

North	East	South	West
1♦	Dbl.	2♠*	Pass
4♠	All Pass		

* Preemptive

Opening lead: **♣ J**

Plan your defense

Given that partner has a singleton spade, it is more than likely that partner is leading from a club sequence as opposed to shortness. Overtake the opening lead and switch to your diamond. Win the ♠A and underlead your life in clubs to partner's ten. Partner's diamond return defeats the contract one trick.

Declarer's hand: ♠ QJ10863 ♥ K96 ♦ 83 ♣ 32
Partner's hand: ♠ 5 ♥ 1075 ♦ 107542 ♣ J1086

WHEN YOU HOLD THE ACE OF TRUMP (A TREASURE)

469* When partner leads a trump from a likely doubleton and finds you with Axx and no outside entries, it is usually right to duck. If partner has a quick entry, partner can return her remaining trump, allowing you to play a second and third round.

470* If dummy has TWO trump and you have Axx(x) plus shortness, win the SECOND round of trump and exit with your short suit putting dummy on play. If declarer cannot conveniently get back to her hand to draw trump, you may get your ruff. Play similarly with Ax of trump when partner has the side suit shortness.

East-West vul.
Dealer South

North (dummy)
♠ Q4
♥ K4
♦ K8762
♣ AKQJ

West
♠ A952
♥ 3
♦ AJ94
♣ 10976

East (you)
♠ J10763
♥ A98
♦ Q53
♣ 83

South
♠ K8
♥ QJ107652
♦ 10
♣ 542

South	West	North	East
3♥	Pass	4♥	All Pass

Opening lead: **♣10**

At trick one start an echo. When the ♥K is played at trick two, duck. Win the second heart and stick dummy back in with a club. Declarer cannot get off dummy safely and you will get your ruff.

471* Underleading Ax of trump may be the only way to stop a ruff in dummy while still retaining control of the hand. This play works best when dummy has two trump and your side has a quick winner in dummy's short suit.

Neither side vul.
Dealer South

North (dummy)
♠ Q8
♥ KJ
♦ A10987
♣ AKJ5

West
♠ 43
♥ 109875
♦ J632
♣ Q2

East (you)
♠ A2
♥ AQ6
♦ KQ4
♣ 109763

South
♠ KJ109765
♥ 432
♦ 5
♣ 84

South	West	North	East
3♠	Pass	4♠	Dbl.
Pass	Pass	Rdbl.	All Pass

Opening lead: **♥10**

Ouch! North isn't kidding around. After winning the opening heart lead with the queen, only one return defeats this contract,your eensy-teensy ♠ 2. If declarer plays a second heart you can win, cash the trump ace and score a third heart trick. Had you played ace and a spade, declarer could throw a heart on dummy's third club winner. Shifting to either minor at trick two is equally futile because it allows declarer to lead a second heart. Now a spade switch is too late.

472* Holding Axx of trump and defending against a hoped for 4-3 trump fit, you may garner an extra trump trick with a long hand force followed by ducking TWO rounds of trump.

Neither side vul.
Dealer North

North (dummy)
♠ Q72
♥ 843
♦ AKJ10
♣ K106

West
♠ 654
♥ J952
♦ 62
♣ 9843

East (you)
♠ A83
♥ AKQ10
♦ 9743
♣ 82

South
♠ KJ109
♥ 75
♦ Q85
♣ AQJ7

North	East	South	West
1♦	1♥	1♠	Pass
2♠	Pass	4♠	All Pass

Opening lead: **♥2**

South winds up in the only game contract that has a chance and ruffs the third heart. When declarer continues with the ♠KJ, partner plays high-low. This trump echo when not seeking a ruff normally shows three trump. Duck twice.

Triumph! Declarer cannot afford to play a third spade lest you cash a heart. If declarer plays on diamonds, partner ruffs. If declarer plays on clubs, do not ruff. Eventually declarer will have to play diamonds allowing partner to ruff.

473* Another technique to destroy a suspected 4-3 trump fit is to give declarer a ruff and a sluff. This works out spectacularly well when trumps are 4-2 and one defender has four trump to a high honor.

Both sides vul.
Dealer North

North (dummy)
♠ A32
♥ AKQ74
♦ AK
♣ 1076

West (you)
♠ 64
♥ J5
♦ 98543
♣ AK43

East
♠ Q875
♥ 10862
♦ 106
♣ QJ2

South
♠ KJ109
♥ 93
♦ QJ72
♣ 985

North	East	South	West
1♥	Pass	1♠	Pass
3♦	Pass	4♦	Pass
4♠	Pass	Pass	Pass

Opening lead: ♣A (A from AK)

Had North bid differently, North-South might have arrived at the superior 3NT, but that's history. Partner plays the ♣Q, promising the ♣J, so you lead a club to the jack and partner returns a club to your king. Here comes your moment. Play a fourth club trying to protect partner's likely four card trump holding. Twist and turn as she may, declarer has to lose another trick. (If declarer ruffs in dummy, partner discards a diamond).

474* When your objective with trump length is to force DECLARER to ruff, but both opponents are void in the "force suit", best defense is to take your trump honor when dummy's LAST trump is played and then continue with the force.

Both sides vul.
Dealer South

North (dummy)
♠ K8
♥ 753
♦ 763
♣ AKJ98

West (you)
♠ -
♥ AKJ
♦ 109542
♣ 76542

East
♠ A5432
♥ Q10874
♦ J8
♣ 3

South
♠ QJ10976
♥ 62
♦ AKQ
♣ Q10

South	West	North	East
1♠	Pass	2♣	Pass
2♠	Pass	3♠	Pass
4♠	All Pass		

Opening lead: ♥**A**

The defense starts with three rounds of hearts, declarer ruffing. At trick four declarer leads a spade to the king, partner discarding. Don't even think of taking this trick. You and declarer each have the same number of trump and your plan is to force declarer to trump again. You cannot force declarer with a heart if you win the first spade, dummy will ruff. Win the second spade and play a heart.

475* Holding Axxx of trump defending against a 4-4 trump fit and NOT having been able to force either hand, win the THIRD round of trump, leaving you with these options:

(1) Playing a fourth trump converting the hand to notrump.

(2) Forcing one hand to ruff which may make it impossible for declarer to return to the other to remove your last trump. Neither option is available if you win an earlier trump lead.

East-West vul. **Dealer North**	**North** (dummy) ♠ 102 ♥ Q1085 ♦ AKQ74 ♣ J2	
West ♠ KQ975 ♥ 4 ♦ J98 ♣ 9854		**East** (you) ♠ J843 ♥ A632 ♦ 63 ♣ AQ10
	South ♠ A6 ♥ KJ97 ♦ 1052 ♣ K763	

North	**East**	**South**	**West**
1♦	Pass	1♥	Pass
2♥	Pass	2NT	Pass
4♥	All Pass		

Opening lead: ♠**K**

Declarer wins the opening lead and continues with the ♥K which you duck. When a low heart is led to dummy's ten, duck again. If declarer plays a third heart, you can win and play a fourth heart. With the hand converted to notrump, declarer can no longer realize a club trick. In fact, no matter what declarer does, you have an answer as long as you duck the first two heart leads.

476* Playing a 5-3 trump fit, declarer may wish to draw exactly two rounds of trump before going about her business. Easier said than done when one defender has Axx of trump. Best defense to countermand this strategy is to win the SECOND round of trump and play a THIRD.

Neither side vul.
Dealer South

North (dummy)
♠ 976
♥ 642
♦ AK42
♣ 832

West
♠ 43
♥ 83
♦ Q1095
♣ QJ965

East (you)
♠ A82
♥ J1097
♦ J86
♣ 1074

South
♠ KQJ105
♥ AKQ5
♦ 73
♣ AK

South	West	North	East
2♣	Pass	2♦	Pass
2♠	Pass	3♠	Pass
4♣	Pass	4♦	Pass
4♥	Pass	5♦	Pass
6♠	All Pass		

Opening lead: ♣Q

Declarer wins and plunks down the ♠K. Win this trick and kiss the slam goodbye. Declarer will draw a second trump and ruff the fourth heart in dummy as you and partner watch (mournfully). If you win the second spade and exit with a third, it is declarer who is mournful; she can no longer rid herself of that *&%$ fourth heart.

WHEN TO GIVE A RUFF AND A SLUFF

In the examples that follow, giving the opponents a ruff and a sluff is the killing defense. Players have been schooled from birth not to give the opponents a ruff and a sluff. However, IF NO TRICKS ARE AVAILABLE IN THE SIDE SUITS, a ruff and a sluff is frequently the ONLY play. Keep that in mind when you read these tips.

477* With Axxx of trump defending against a 4-4 trump fit, giving the opponents a ruff and a sluff and then winning the THIRD round of trump followed by another force leaves you with the last trump.

Neither side vul.
Dealer South

North (dummy)
♠ KJ95
♥ J5
♦ AQ10
♣ QJ43

West (you)
♠ A842
♥ AK1098
♦ 83
♣ 92

East
♠ 3
♥ Q432
♦ 97642
♣ 1075

South
♠ Q1076
♥ 76
♦ KJ5
♣ AK108

South	West	North	East
1♣	1♥	Dbl*	3♥**
Pass	Pass	Dbl***	Pass
3♠	Pass	4♠	All Pass

* Negative
** Preemptive (no kidding)
*** Strong negative double

Opening lead: ♥**K**

Start with THREE rounds of hearts. Even though you know you are giving the opponents a ruff and a sluff, you also know that you will leave them with a 4-3 trump fit. If declarer begins to draw trump, win the THIRD round and play a fourth heart for down two. If declarer refuses to play a third trump, you will ruff a minor suit winner for down one.

478* Voiding partner in a suit (even if it means giving declarer a ruff and a sluff) with the eventual idea of promoting a trump trick is a great way to get your name in lights.

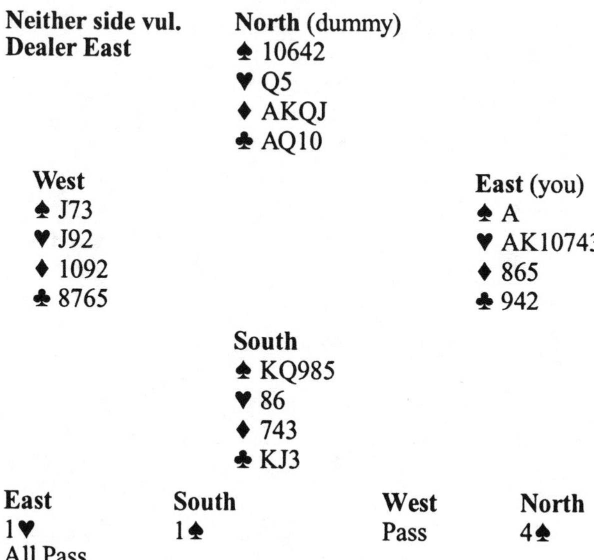

Neither side vul.
Dealer East

North (dummy)
♠ 10642
♥ Q5
♦ AKQJ
♣ AQ10

West
♠ J73
♥ J92
♦ 1092
♣ 8765

East (you)
♠ A
♥ AK10743
♦ 865
♣ 942

South
♠ KQ985
♥ 86
♦ 743
♣ KJ3

East	**South**	**West**	**North**
1♥	1♠	Pass	4♠
All Pass			

Opening lead: ♥**2**

With no minor suit tricks available, the best chance is to play three rounds of hearts and then a fourth heart upon winning the ♠A in hopes of promoting a trump trick for partner. In this case, partner's "projected" ♠J becomes the setting trick.

479* Strange and wonderful secondary trump promotions exist when you can lead a suit partner doesn't have—even if it means giving the opponents a ruff and a sluff.

North-South vul.
Dealer South

North (dummy)
♠ J8
♥ A72
♦ K103
♣ KQ654

West
♠ 652
♥ Q83
♦ Q8754
♣ 87

East (you)
♠ AK10943
♥ K4
♦ 92
♣ 1093

South
♠ Q7
♥ J10965
♦ AJ6
♣ AJ2

South	**West**	**North**	**East**
1♥	Pass	2♣	2♠
Pass	Pass	4♥	All Pass

Opening lead: **♠2**

Looking at all four hands it may be difficult to see how four hearts can be beaten, but it can. Say you start with THREE rounds of spades. Declarer ruffs and runs the ♥J to your king. Now a fourth spade from you promotes a trump trick for partner. If declarer doesn't ruff, partner uppercuts dummy with the ♥8; if declarer ruffs high, partner discards, once again promoting the ♥8 to master rank.

480* Giving the opponents a ruff and a sluff may be a blessing in disguise if it gives partner an opportunity to make a killing discard.

Both sides vul.
Dealer West

North (dummy)
♠ KQJ10
♥ KQ876
♦ J4
♣ AK

West (you)
♠ 8
♥ A10
♦ AK87653
♣ QJ8

East
♠ A52
♥ 93
♦ 109
♣ 975432

South
♠ 97643
♥ J542
♦ Q2
♣ 106

West	**North**	**East**	**South**
1♦	Dbl.	Pass	1♠
3♦	3♠	All Pass	

Opening lead: ♦A

* After cashing two diamonds, why not try a third? If partner has ♠A9x your play promotes the ♠9. (Partner doesn't overtrump dummy, but later puts you in with the ♥A to play a fourth diamond). Another possibility is to hope partner has a doubleton heart. Your third diamond play allows her to discard a high heart. When partner gets in with the ♠A, she can return her lower heart and get a ruff.

* When giving declarer a ruff and a sluff, lead your HIGHEST remaining card, here the ♦8, so partner will know what you are doing. If you lead a lower diamond, partner will think that declarer has a higher diamond and will certainly err.

481* When faced with a choice of leading a side suit that will establish an extra trick for declarer or giving declarer a ruff and a sluff, give the ruff and sluff.

East-West vul.
Dealer North

North (dummy)
♠ KJ98
♥ A76
♦ 2
♣ AKJ65

West (you)
♠ 32
♥ 95432
♦ AQ1087
♣ 3

East
♠ 54
♥ QJ10
♦ 543
♣ Q10982

South
♠ AQ1076
♥ K8
♦ KJ96
♣ 74

North	East	South	West
1♣	Pass	1♠	Pass
3♦*	Pass	4NT	Pass
5♥	Pass	6♠	All Pass

* Splinter

Opening lead: **♣3**

Declarer wins the opening lead, draws two rounds of trump, strips the hearts and leads a club to dummy's ace getting the bad news. When declarer follows with a diamond to the jack and queen you are on lead with an apparent choice of evils. You can give declarer a ruff and a sluff or you can lead a diamond into declarer's likely king. No choice. Lead a heart. After the heart switch, declarer has no play.

482* When defending against a two-suiter, giving declarer a ruff and a sluff when declarer has no side suit loser may prevent declarer from establishing the side suit.

Neither side vul.
Dealer West

North (dummy)
♠ 10987
♥ 32
♦ K865
♣ Q103

West
♠ A3
♥ Q1084
♦ Q107
♣ K852

East (you)
♠ J2
♥ K9
♦ 9432
♣ AJ976

South
♠ KQ654
♥ AJ765
♦ AJ
♣ 4

West	**North**	**East**	**South**
Pass	Pass	Pass	1♠
Dbl.	2♠	3♣	4♠
All Pass			

Opening lead: **♣2**

Declarer ruffs the second round of clubs and exits with the ♠K. Partner wins and forces declarer with a club. Declarer draws trump and exits with a low heart to your nine. The only return to defeat the contract is a fourth club. Wiggle as she may, declarer can no longer establish the fifth heart.

483. When partner gives the opponents a ruff and a sluff, don't give birth at the table; partner is planning a trump promotion of sorts. (Either that or you should be looking for a new partner).

TRUMP PROMOTION PLAYS

484. When partner is void in a suit, a trump promotion play may be available by leading that suit. In each of the following diagrams assume the suit you see is spades, the trump suit. PRETEND you are leading some suit partner doesn't have (even if you are giving the opponents a ruff and a sluff), and watch the wonderful things that can happen.

(a) **North** (dummy)
AKQ

West (you)
4

East
J65

South
1098732

Here you promote partner's jack.

(b) **North** (dummy)
2

West
9643

East (you)
J

South
AKQ10875

Here you promote partner's nine.

(c) **North** (dummy)
QJ105

West
83

East (you)
K92

South
A764

This is an interesting one. Partner ruffs with the eight driving out the ten and your K92 is now a natural trump trick. This one works equally well if partner leads a suit in which you are void. If dummy ruffs high, discard and your ♠9 is a third round winner; if dummy doesn't ruff, ruff with the nine to promote your king.

485* Forcing partner to trump high (the good old "uppercut") is a tried and true method of promoting extra trump tricks for yourself. In the following diagrams the suit you see is spades, the trump suit, and you are leading a suit that neither partner nor declarer has. In addition, your partner has been programmed to trump high in these positions.

(a)

	North (dummy) 75	
West(you) K92		**East** 103
	South AQJ864	

Partner ruffs with the ten and your K92 is now worth two tricks.

On a good day you can force partner to ruff high TWICE in the same suit.

(b)

	North (dummy) None	
West(you) A72		**East** 984
	South KQJ10653	

Partner ruffs with the eight driving out an honor. You win the first trump lead and lead the "uppercut" suit again. This time partner trumps with the nine. Don't look now but your seven is a third round winner.

486* When you are in a position to overtrump a known strong trump holding, check to see whether you have any interesting trump intermediates before rushing the net with an overruff. As often as not, you save a trick by not overtrumping.

	North (dummy) 4	
West (you) Q932		**East** 54
	South AKJ1087	

Partner leads a suit in which both you and declarer are void. If declarer ruffs with the ten or jack, you get two tricks if you don't overruff, one if you do. There are many similar positions.

If it can be right not to overtrump declarer, it can also be right not to overtrump dummy.

North (dummy)
QJ9

West
2

East (you)
K108

South
A76543

If partner leads a suit in which both you and dummy are void and dummy trumps high, you get two tricks if you DON'T overtrump; one if you do.

488* Playing equal honors out of order, asks partner to unblock. This, in turn, may lead to a trump promotion

Neither side vul.
Dealer South

North (dummy)
♠ 92
♥ AK65
♦ 854
♣ AK103

West
♠ J65
♥ 10832
♦ Q32
♣ Q97

East (you)
♠ 8
♥ 974
♦ AKJ7
♣ J8652

South
♠ AKQ10743
♥ QJ
♦ 1096
♣ 4

South	West	North	East
1♠	Pass	2♣	Pass
2♠	Pass	3♥	Pass
4♠	All Pass		

Opening lead: ♦2

To get a gold star, play the ace and then the king of diamonds to the first two tricks. Playing equal honors out of order either shows a doubleton or asks partner to unblock. Given the bidding, partner should assume diamond length and unblock the queen. Now a third and fourth diamond promote the ♠J to the setting trick.

489* Are you ready for the longest tip in the book? If not, move right along. When deciding whether to lead a suit through declarer that neither partner nor declarer has, a suit in which you have the master card but dummy has the next highest, ask yourself:
(1) How strong are partner's trumps?
(2) Does dummy have any outside entries?
(3) Does declarer have any outside losers?
(4) Can you cash your outside winners first?
(5) Can you can kill an eventual winner by leading low?
(6) Is it possible the suit should not be led at all?
(7) How many more tricks do I need to defeat this contract?

Keep in mind that if you lead high, you set up one or more winners in dummy. If you lead low, declarer can discard a loser. So what is the tip already?
(A) If partner has worthless trump, lead LOW.
(B) If the idea is to kill an eventual ruffing finesse, lead LOW.
(C) If dummy has no side entry lead HIGH.
(D) If the discard(s) will be of no value to the declarer, lead HIGH.
(E) If you need ONE trump promotion, cash your outside winners first and then lead HIGH OR LOW.
(F) If you have quick outside entry (an ace) in a "safe" suit (a suit that declarer cannot profitably discard), lead HIGH. This may give you a chance for a second trump promotion.
(G) If you can't cash your outside winners and partner is likely to have a natural trump trick (and there is an outside dummy entry), DON'T LEAD THE SUIT AT ALL.

Of course, by this time it doesn't matter what you do, everyone has gone home.

Neither side vul.
Dealer North

North (dummy)
♠ A74
♥ Q1054
♦ KQ3
♣ QJ10

East (you)
♠ 53
♥ KJ986
♦ AJ106
♣ 75

North	**East**	**South**	**West**
1♣	1♥	1♠	Pass
1NT	Pass	3♣	Pass
4♠	All Pass		

Opening lead: **♥A**
Partner continues a second heart to the ten and jack. Now what?

Cash your diamond winner before leading a heart, any heart. (You need only one trump promotion and declarer is likely to have a singleton diamond). Once all side winners have been cashed it no longer matters whether you lead high or low. Here it is slightly better to lead a low heart in case declarer is 6-4 in the blacks and partner has the ♣K. (Case E)

Declarer's hand: ♠ KQ1086 ♥ 73 ♦ 8 ♣ AK964
Partner's hand: ♠ J92 ♥ A2 ♦ 97542 ♣ 832

If you lead a heart, any heart, BEFORE you cash the ♦A, the hand can no longer be defeated. If you lead a low heart, declarer will discard a diamond; if you lead a high heart, declarer will ruff high, draw two trump and discard her singleton diamond on the ♥Q.

East-West vul.
Dealer East

North (dummy)
♠ KJ10
♥ K32
♦ J987
♣ AK10

East (you)
♠ A32
♥ 4
♦ KQ653
♣ QJ98

East	**South**	**West**	**North**
1♦	2♥	Pass	3♦*
Pass	3♥	All Pass	

* Game try in hearts
Opening lead: ♦A

Partner continues with a second diamond which you win with the queen, declarer following twice. Now what?

It is fair to assume that declarer has six hearts and is known to have two diamonds, leaving declarer with five black cards. Given that declarer cannot have a singleton spade (partner with six spades plus the ♦A would have peeped), declarer has only one black suit loser. As that loser cannot get away, lead the ♦K. If partner can overruff declarer, and then overruff declarer again after putting you on lead with the ♠A, your primo defense might have been the only defense. (Case F)

Declarer's hand: ♠ Q85 ♥ AJ9765 ♦ 102 ♣ 73

Partner's hand: ♠ 9764 ♥ Q108 ♦ A4 ♣ 6542

Neither side vul.
Dealer West

North (dummy)
♠ A84
♥ Q1093
♦ 1094
♣ KJ6

East (you)
♠ J109
♥ KJ87652
♦ A
♣ 75

West	**North**	**East**	**South**
Pass	Pass	3♥	4♦
Pass	5♦	All Pass	

Opening lead: ♥ A

Declarer wins the club shift with the ace and leads a high diamond to your ace. Your play?

In order to kill the threat of an eventual ruffing finesse in hearts, lead a LOW heart while partner still has a trump. (case B)

Declarer's hand: ♠ Q5 ♥ 4 ♦ KQJ8765 ♣ AQ4
Partner's hand: ♠ K7632 ♥ A ♦ 32 ♣ 109832

Neither side vul.
Dealer South

North (dummy)
♠ Q832
♥ A53
♦ K76
♣ AJ6

East (you)
♠ KJ976
♥ 4
♦ QJ105
♣ K83

South	**West**	**North**	**East**
2♥	Pass	Pass	2♠
Pass	Pass	3♥	All Pass

Opening lead: ♠A

Partner continues with a second spade which you win with the jack, declarer following. What now?

Don't play a spade. Partner is apt to have a trump winner and declarer's minor suit losers are "slow" (you must wait for them). Exit with the ♦Q and play the waiting game.

Declarer's hand: ♠ 105 ♥ KJ9862 ♦ A84 ♣ 94
Partner's hand: ♠ A4 ♥ Q107 ♦ 932 ♣ Q10752

If you show patience and exit with a diamond you will eventually get a trick in each minor along with a trump trick for down one. If you lead a spade, any spade, at trick three, the contract is made easily. (Case G)

490* When trying to promote an extra trump trick for yourself by giving partner a chance to uppercut, cash any side suit winner(s) that might vanish before going for the uppercut.

East-West vul.
Dealer South

North (dummy)
♠ KQJ
♥ 54
♦ K8764
♣ J73

West (you)
♠ 963
♥ K92
♦ A92
♣ Q1062

East
♠ 10874
♥ 103
♦ J1073
♣ AK8

South
♠ A52
♥ AQJ876
♦ Q
♣ 954

South	**West**	**North**	**East**
1♥	Pass	1NT	Pass
2♥	All Pass		

Opening lead: **♣2**

Partner wins the ♣AK and plays a third to your queen. Your best chance is to cash the ♦A and lead a fourth club. If partner can ruff with an honor (any honor) your trump holding is good for two tricks. (Nines when attached to a higher honor become big cards when partner uppercuts). If you fail to cash the ♦A, declarer can succeed by discarding a diamond when partner uppercuts.

491* When you want partner to uppercut in a suit partner knows you have the high cards, lead low, an UPPERCUT DEMAND. If you lead high, you are telling partner NOT to uppercut.

Both sides vul.
Dealer South

North (dummy)
♠ KQ42
♥ J76
♦ -
♣ AKJ876

West (you)
♠ 93
♥ AKQ984
♦ 1053
♣ Q4

East
♠ 10875
♥ 103
♦ Q4
♣ 109532

South
♠ AJ6
♥ 52
♦ AKJ98762
♣ -

South	West	North	East
1♦	1♥	2♣	Pass
3♦	Pass	3♠	Pass
5♦	All Pass		

Opening lead: ♥Q (Q from AKQ asking for count)

After you cash two hearts, lead a low heart and hope partner has a trump honor to play. If she does, your innocuous ♦10 becomes the setting trick. A clear case of a frog turning into a prince.

492* Playing high-low feigning a doubleton when dummy has a doubleton and partner has led from the ace-king may provoke declarer into ruffing the third round high. This, in turn, may promote a trump trick for your side.

East West vul.
Dealer South

North (dummy)
♠ A86
♥ J10
♦ AKJ3
♣ KQJ6

West
♠ -
♥ AK743
♦ 10752
♣ 7532

East (you)
♠ 10975
♥ 982
♦ Q94
♣ A108

South
♠ KQJ432
♥ Q65
♦ 86
♣ 94

South	West	North	East
2♠	Pass	4♠	All Pass

Opening lead: **♥A**

Given the strength of this dummy, the only real hope is to try to convince declarer you have a doubleton heart. If you play the ♥9 and partner continues the king and a heart, declarer has a problem. If you have a doubleton, declarer must ruff with the ♠A. If declarer falls for your ruse, you wind up with the setting trick in the trump suit.

WHEN IT IS WISE NOT TO SHORTEN DECLARER.

493* "Natural" trump tricks can vanish if declarer can reduce to your length, throw you in with a trump and force a trump return. To avoid this embarrassment, don't lead any suit that declarer can ruff.

North (dummy)
-

West (you)
J9765

East
2

South
AKQ10843

This is the trump suit and you appear to have two certain winners, but you DON'T. If declarer can ruff TWICE, strip you of your outside cards and exit with a small trump (after having played the AK), you will have to win and return a trump. Suddenly your two "certain" trump tricks have turned into one.

494* When there is a strong possibility that declarer can trump coup you: (1) do not shorten declarer; (2) try to drive out dummy entries before declarer discovers the bad trump break.

Neither side vul.
Dealer South

North (dummy)
♠ AK1043
♥ K4
♦ 8763
♣ Q5

West
♠ J87
♥ 3
♦ A1094
♣ 109862

East (you)
♠ Q92
♥ A1082
♦ KQJ
♣ 753

South
♠ 65
♥ QJ9765
♦ 52
♣ AKJ

South	West	North	East
1♥	Pass	1♠	Pass
2♥	Pass	4♥	All Pass

Opening lead: ♣10

Declarer wins the ♣K and leads a trump to the king and ace. Although it is VERY tempting to switch to a diamond (partner probably has the ace), a club return is better. Declarer's diamond loser(s) aren't going away. By shortening declarer you harm your own cause. Declarer will ruff the third diamond and play a high trump getting the bad news. No problem, declarer plays the ace-king and ruffs a spade, reducing to your length, crosses to a club and plays a high spade. It does you no good to ruff, so you discard and so does declarer. Don't look now, but declarer is in dummy and her last two cards are the ♥J9 sitting over your ♥108. If you return a club at trick three, removing a vital dummy entry, declarer's trump coup isn't.

WHEN NOT TO RUFF

495* Don't ruff air! When declarer leads a low card in a side suit towards the closed hand preparatory to ruffing that suit in dummy, and you, second hand, are void and have trump that can overtrump dummy, do NOT ruff. You will be ruffing a loser with a winner, a gigantic no-no.

Both sides vul.
Dealer South

North (dummy)
♠ 973
♥ K2
♦ A976
♣ Q762

West
♠ 64
♥ QJ973
♦ 104
♣ J1093

East (you)
♠ 1082
♥ 5
♦ QJ852
♣ AK84

South
♠ AKQJ5
♥ A10864
♦ K3
♣ 5

South	**West**	**North**	**East**
1♠	Pass	2♠	Pass
4♠	All Pass		

Opening lead: ♣J

Declarer ruffs the second club and leads a heart to the king and another heart. If you ruff, declarer makes the contract with ease. Declarer ruffs your club return, draws two trump and then ruffs a heart in dummy for the tenth trick. However, if you discard on the second heart, declarer cannot avoid losing three more heart tricks. If declarer draws trump, partner has three heart winners; if declarer tries to trump hearts, you can overtrump twice and return a trump preventing declarer from ruffing a third heart.

496* When declarer has NO side suit losers, yet insists upon leading winners from dummy through you before drawing trump, you should smell a large rat. Declarer is trying to bait you into trumping so she can locate the trump queen. DO NOT RUFF.

North-South vul.
Dealer East

North (dummy)
♠ K76
♥ AK74
♦ A
♣ KJ743

East (you)
♠ 82
♥ 3
♦ J87542
♣ 10962

East	**South**	**West**	**North**
Pass	1♠	4♥	5♥
Pass	6♠	Pass	7♠
All Pass			

Opening lead: ♥Q

Declarer wins in dummy pitching a club. At trick two declarer leads another high heart. What do you do?

Don't ruff! Declarer has no club losers. If partner had the ♣A, she would have led it. Declarer is trying to smoke out the spade queen by suckering you into using a small trump.

Declarer's hand: ♠ AJ10954 ♥ - ♦ K93 ♣ AQ85
Partner's hand: ♠ Q3 ♥ QJ1098652 ♦ Q106 ♣ -

TRAPS TO AVOID

497* Beware of Greeks bearing gifts—in this case a declarer who presents you with a trump trick you never had coming.

Both vul.
Dealer South

North (dummy)
♠ 1062
♥ AK87
♦ 865
♣ 732

East (you)
♠ J73
♥ Q1062
♦ 92
♣ QJ105

South	**West**	**North**	**East**
2♣ *	Pass	2♦**	Pass
2♠	Pass	3♠	Pass
6♠	All Pass		

* Strong and artificial
** Waiting

Opening lead: ♦Q

Declarer wins the ♦A and plays the ♠A, partner discarding a low heart. At trick two declarer leads the ♠9, partner discarding the ♦7 (present count). Has declarer gone mad? No, but you will if you win this trick. Declarer is clearly void in hearts and is trying desperately to create a trump entry to dummy.

Declarer's hand: ♠ AKQ9854 ♥ - ♦ AK3 ♣ AK4
Partner's hand: ♠ - ♥ J9543 ♦ QJ1074 ♣ 986

498* When there is a good chance that declarer is void in dummy's strong suit, hang on to your lowest trump for dear life. If you don't, something terrible may happen.

North-South vul.
Dealer East

North (dummy)
♠ 3
♥ AKQ753
♦ 643
♣ 753

West
♠ 2
♥ 6
♦ QJ1097
♣ QJ9842

East (you)
♠ 10764
♥ J109842
♦ 8
♣ 106

South
♠ AKQJ985
♥ -
♦ AK52
♣ AK

East	South	West	North
Pass	2♣	2NT*	4♥
Pass	6♠	All Pass	

* Minors

Opening lead: ♦Q

Declarer wins and plays the ♠AK, partner discarding a club. Are you organized? It won't matter how organized you are if you have already parted with your ♠4. Declarer will play a third trump followed by two top clubs and second high diamond. If you ruff, you must put dummy on play with a heart. If you don't ruff, declarer ever so gently leads a LOW spade to your ten forcing you to lead a heart. In order to beat the slam you must clutch that ♠4 for dear life. If you do, declarer will wind up stuck in her hand with two losing diamonds.

499. If it is clear that declarer is desperately trying to get back to her hand to repeat a trump finesse that works, your job is not to let her.

Both vul.
Dealer North

North (dummy)
♠ AQJ
♥ KJ542
♦ AK
♣ 642

West
♠ K92
♥ A3
♦ 95432
♣ 1095

East (you)
♠ 3
♥ 10876
♦ QJ107
♣ KQJ8

South
♠ 1087654
♥ Q9
♦ 86
♣ A73

North	**East**	**South**	**West**
1♥	Pass	1♠	Pass
3♠	Pass	4♠	All Pass

Opening lead: ♣10

Declarer wins the second club, leads a trump to the jack, cashes the ♦AK, partner showing an odd number, and exits with a heart to the queen and ace. When partner returns a club you are on play holding three hearts, two diamonds and a club. There is only one card you can play to defeat the contract, the ♥10. This stuffs declarer in dummy. No matter what declarer does now, a spade must be lost to the king. Yes, declarer should have exited with a club instead of leading a heart at trick six, but that's not your problem.

500. When declarer is leading winners through you and you have a high trump and a low trump and dummy to your left has a middle trump... misery. So what's the tip? Consider discarding; you may be able to ruff the suit you are discarding later.

Both sides vul.
Dealer South

North (dummy)
♠ A64
♥ AQ876
♦ K5
♣ 1043

West (you)
♠ Q1052
♥ K3
♦ 876
♣ AJ52

East
♠ KJ987
♥ J1042
♦ 1043
♣ 6

South
♠ 3
♥ 95
♦ AQJ92
♣ KQ987

South	**West**	**North**	**East**
1♦	Pass	1♥	Pass
2♣	Pass	2♠	Pass
3♣	Pass	3♦	Pass
3♥	Pass	4♣	Pass
5♣	All Pass		

Opening lead: ♠2

At trick two declarer leads a club to the king which you routinely duck. Declarer crosses to the ♦K and leads a low club to the nine and jack, partner discarding a spade. You tap declarer with a spade reducing her trump length to your trump length, two each. Declarer fights back by playing winning diamonds through you. Rather than ruff, discard both of your hearts. Soon declarer will realize she should have finessed and cashed two hearts BEFORE playing diamonds. Now it is too late. As declarer cannot afford to play a third trump for fear of a spade force, she will have to play a heart which you can ruff.

501. When declarer is desperately shortening her trump holding with the idea of a trump endplay, don't forget a counter: The underruff. Why shouldn't you make a spectacular play once in a while?

North-South vul.
Dealer South

North (dummy)
♠ 32
♥ K1076
♦ KJ6
♣ 8532

West (you)
♠ J976
♥ 854
♦ 1087
♣ 764

East
♠ 4
♥ QJ9
♦ 9432
♣ KQJ109

South
♠ AKQ1085
♥ A32
♦ AQ5
♣ A

South	West	North	East
2♣	Pass	2♦*	3♣
3♠	Pass	4♠**	Pass
6♠	All Pass		

* Waiting
** Shows some strength- 4♣ by agreement would have been the double negative.

Opening lead: ♣4

Declarer plunks down the ace and king of spades getting the bad news and the play suddenly slows to a crawl. Declarer emerges from her shell with a plan. She play the ace-king of hearts and ruffs a club low. She crosses to the ♦J and ruffs another club low. (She has now reduced to your trump length). Not content yet, declarer cashes the ace and king of diamonds followed by ruffing a club high. At this point you have three spades and a losing heart. If you discard your losing heart, declarer will lead a heart which you will have to ruff and, worse, lead a spade from your J9 into the waiting clutches of her Q10. However, if you underruff, partner will win the heart exit and your ♠J will be the setting trick. Get on the phone, call your friends, call the newspaper.

502* When dummy is entryless, don't play the role of the good Samaritan, particularly when exiting with a trump.

North (dummy)
8

West (you)
932

East
75

South
AKQJ1064

If you think your safest exit is a trump, and you fear dummy is entryless, exit with the nine. Better safe than sorry.

MISCELLANEOUS TRUMP SUIT PLAYS

503* When you have the HIGH trump(s) (partner has none), and you are on lead, cash the high trump(s) UNLESS your trump holding prevents declarer from running a side suit.

East-West vul.
Dealer South

North (dummy)
♠ 63
♥ J95
♦ KQ1087
♣ J54

West (you)
♠ QJ52
♥ 763
♦ 96
♣ AK87

East
♠ 4
♥ KQ84
♦ 5432
♣ Q1032

South
♠ AK10987
♥ A102
♦ AJ
♣ 96

South	West	North	East
1♠	Pass	1NT	Pass
3♠	All Pass		

Opening lead: ♣ A

You start with three rounds of clubs, declarer ruffing. Declarer continues with ace, king, and a spade, partner playing an encouraging heart and a discouraging diamond. Do not cash your high trump, it is your diamond stopper! Shift to a heart. Declarer no longer can get rid of her heart loser in time (you will ruff the third diamond).

504. When you have the high trump and declarer has one lower trump, but declarer has the lead and begins to cash winners in dummy's long suit, use your trump when declarer is playing her LAST card in dummy's suit.

East-West vul.
Dealer West

North (dummy)
♠ 87
♥ 864
♦ KQ943
♣ Q75

West (you)
♠ J432
♥ AKQ92
♦ -
♣ KJ92

East
♠ 65
♥ 1073
♦ J865
♣ 10864

South
♠ AKQ109
♥ J5
♦ AJ72
♣ A3

West	**North**	**East**	**South**
1♥	Pass	Pass	Dbl.
2♣	2♦	3♣	4♠
All Pass			

Opening lead: ♥Q (Q from AKQ)

Declarer ruffs the third heart, cashes three rounds of spades, partner discarding a low club, and begins to cash diamond winners. To defeat the contract, you must discard two clubs and a heart on the first three diamond plays and ruff the FOURTH. After you exit a heart, declarer must lose a club.

505* When holding a finessable trump honor, forcing dummy to ruff may give your trump honor a new life.

North (dummy)
J42

West
8

East (you)
K763

South
AQ1095

If you can force dummy to ruff, you stand an excellent chance of scoring a trump trick.

506. When declarer begins to discard losers BEFORE drawing trump, the inference is that the trump suit is leaky; otherwise why not draw trump first?

507* With worthless trump, you can foil a "loser on loser" by ruffing the first equal.

North-South vul.
Dealer South

North (dummy)
♠ QJ62
♥ J104
♦ 432
♣ 976

West
♠ K1098753
♥ 2
♦ KQ10
♣ 82

East (you)
♠ 4
♥ 753
♦ J985
♣ KQJ104

South
♠ A
♥ AKQ986
♦ A76
♣ A53

South	West	North	East
2♣	3♠	Dbl.*	Pass
4♥	All Pass		

* Denying any ace or king by agreement.

Opening lead: ♦K (A from AK)

You signal encouragement and declarer, thinking longingly of 3NT, wins the ace, cashes both major suit aces and enters dummy with a heart. At trick five the ♠Q is led from dummy. If you discard allowing partner to win the trick, declarer will eventually discard a losing club on the ♠J. If you ruff the ♠Q, there will be no later discard.

508* If you need partner to have a high trump honor in order to defeat the contact, assume she has it. It might be:
(1) A trump honor that can be used to uppercut declarer.
(2) A trump honor that can be promoted by putting partner in a favorable overruff position.
(3) A trump honor that can be promoted by giving declarer a ruff and a sluff.
(4) A possible entry to get a ruff.

(14)
DEFENSE TO ENDPLAYS

When declarer can draw trump and remain with trump in each hand, bad things in the form of endplays or throw-ins may be in your future. This is what you must be on the lookout for:

(1) Declarer has losers in TWO suits and uses one suit as a THROW-IN suit to force a lead in another (the CRITICAL suit).

(2) Declarer has losers in only ONE suit, the "critical" suit.

Best defense requires a recognition of both suits plus knowing how many tricks are needed from the critical suit when the moment of truth arrives .

THE CRITICAL SUIT

509* When a hand has been stripped and declarer has losers in only one suit, play second hand high with honor doubleton or unblock with honor doubleton in fourth seat when declarer finally gets around to the critical suit.

East-West vul.
Dealer South

North (dummy)
♠ KQ742
♥ KQ
♦ 732
♣ AK8

West
♠ 4
♥ A1084
♦ AJ105
♣ QJ106

East (you)
♠ 3
♥ J7653
♦ Q6
♣ 97432

South
♠ AJ10965
♥ 92
♦ K984
♣ 5

South	**West**	**North**	**East**
2♠	Dbl.	4♠	All Pass

Opening lead: ♣Q

At trick two declarer crosses to a trump and leads a heart. Partner wins and exits with a club honor to dummy, declarer discarding a diamond. A club is ruffed, dummy is entered with a heart and a diamond is led. Rise and shine. Play the queen to unblock the suit. Your side needs three diamond tricks and you must play partner for the AJ10 (or the AK). If you play low, declarer will duck the trick into partner who will be endplayed. (Even if declarer drunkenly plays the king, your queen blocks the suit and you must give declarer a ruff and a sluff).

Both sides vul.
Dealer North

North (dummy)
♠ K8754
♥ 9
♦ AJ9
♣ KJ62

West
♠ A106
♥ 10875
♦ KQ84
♣ 53

East (you)
♠ J3
♥ QJ632
♦ 107532
♣ 8

South
♠ Q92
♥ AK4
♦ 6
♣ AQ10974

North	East	South	West
1♠	Pass	2♣	Pass
3♣	Pass	3♠	Pass
4♦	Pass	4♥	Pass
5♣	Pass	6♣	All Pass

Opening lead: ♦K

Declarer wins the opening lead in dummy, ruffs a diamond high, draws trump, strips the red suits and eventually leads a spade to the king. Unblock the jack! If you don't, you get one spade trick instead of two. Play the same with ♠Qx in case partner has A10x.

(a) **North**
Axx
West **Q10xxx**
East (you) **Kx**
South
Jxx

(b) **North**
Axx
West **K10xxx**
East (you) **Qx**
South
Jxx

Assume this is the ORIGINAL distribution of the critical suit and the hand has been stripped OR IS ABOUT TO BE and declarer cashes dummy's ace. In both cases dump your honor under the ace to avoid blocking the suit. It only hurts for a little while.

510* After a hand has been stripped and declarer leads the critical suit from weakness towards strength, second hand must often play high from 10xx, Jxx(x) or Qxx(x) to prevent declarer from ducking the trick into partner.

Neither side vul.
Dealer South

North (dummy)
♠ J1076
♥ Q6
♦ 843
♣ KQ105

West
♠ 32
♥ AKJ87
♦ AQ102
♣ 94

East (you)
♠ 95
♥ 95432
♦ J76
♣ 832

South
♠ AKQ84
♥ 10
♦ K95
♣ AJ76

South	**West**	**North**	**East**
1♠	2♥	2♠	Pass
4♠	All Pass		

Opening lead: ♥A

Hard to believe that you are about to be the heroine of this hand, isn't it?

Partner continues with a second high heart which declarer ruffs. Trumps are drawn, clubs stripped and a diamond led from dummy. Play the jack. Your side needs THREE diamond tricks to defeat the contract. You must project the AQ10x in partner's hand. If you play low, declarer will insert the nine endplaying partner.

511* When a hand has been stripped and you need TWO tricks from the critical suit and RHO leads low from the ace, play low in second seat holding the king with ANY length... without dithering.

	North (dummy)	
	A65	
West		**East** (you)
J10743		K2
	South	
	Q98	

If North leads low, play low. If declarer plays your partner for the king, she will insert the nine and duck partner's return.

512* When YOU are the one that is forced to lead the critical suit and you need but ONE trick in the suit, lead:

(1) low from Kx(x)(x).
(2) low from Jx(x)(x) or Q(x)(x) if you cannot see either the ace or the king in dummy or you can see them both.
(3) lead your honor from Jx(x)(x) or Qx(x)(x) if you see either the ace or the king in the dummy.
(4) lead low from Jx(x)(x) if you see the queen in dummy.

513* One way to break up an endplay is to ask partner to lead the critical suit early before declarer can strip the hand.

North-South vul.	**North** (dummy)	
Dealer East	♠ Q4	
	♥ AQ42	
	♦ AQ10	
	♣ KJ98	
West		**East** (you)
♠ A86		♠ J109753
♥ 86		♥ K53
♦ 9753		♦ KJ6
♣ 7432		♣ 5
	South	
	♠ K2	
	♥ J1097	
	♦ 842	
	♣ AQ106	

East	**South**	**West**	**North**
2♠	Pass	3♠	Dbl.
Pass	4♥	All Pass	

Opening lead: ♠ A

Play the ♠J (suit preference when your bidding has shown a six card suit or longer-tip 151). If partner shifts to a diamond, declarer is doomed to lose two diamonds, a spade and a heart. If partner does not shift to a diamond, declarer can strip the hand and lead a diamond to the ten, endplaying you.

WHEN YOU HAVE BEEN THROWN IN

514* If either defender can take the trick in the throw-in suit, the defender who can attack the critical suit to best advantage shall be the "chosen".

East-West vul.
Dealer North

North (dummy)
♠ A4
♥ Q1094
♦ 8632
♣ K85

West (you)
♠ KQ93
♥ 65
♦ A105
♣ 10764

East
♠ J8752
♥ 72
♦ QJ9
♣ 932

South
♠ 106
♥ AKJ83
♦ K74
♣ AQ2

North	**East**	**South**	**West**
Pass	Pass	1♥	Pass
3♥	Pass	4♥	All Pass

Opening lead: ♠K

Declarer wins the ace, draws trump, strips the clubs and exits with the ♠10. Lesser players (not you), might win the ♠Q fearing declarer has the ♠J. However, if declarer has the ♠J, the contract is unbeatable because declarer can have no more than two diamonds. On the other hand, if partner has the needed ♠J, diamonds may have to be led through declarer. If the declarer leads the second spade from dummy, partner must step up smartly with the jack.

515* If you have the foresight to visualize the throw-in suit and know that it will be better for you to be leading the critical suit, save at least one high card in the likely throw-in suit.

Neither side vul.
Dealer West

North (dummy)
♠ AK3
♥ AQ42
♦ AKQ5
♣ A9

West
♠ 105
♥ K53
♦ 6
♣ KQ108765

East (you)
♠ QJ8762
♥ 1098
♦ 93
♣ J2

South
♠ 94
♥ J76
♦ J108742
♣ 43

West	**North**	**East**	**South**
3♣	Dbl.	Pass	3♦
Pass	4♣	Pass	4♦
Pass	6♦	All Pass	

Opening lead: ♣K

Although it is usually right to echo with a doubleton, it isn't here. After winning the ♣A, drawing trump and stripping spades, declarer exits with a club. If partner wins the trick, she is end-played. She must either break hearts or give declarer a ruff and a sluff. Either switch is a disaster. However, if YOU win the second club lead, you can safely exit a heart to defeat the slam.

516* If you can see far enough ahead to recognize which is the throw-in suit and which is the critical suit, and also that it is vital for PARTNER to be on lead after the throw-in, then it is up to you to make sure partner keeps a high honor in the throw-in suit.

Both sides vul.
Dealer South

North (dummy)
♠ K3
♥ A10985
♦ 1098
♣ 1098

West (you)
♠ J1092
♥ K2
♦ QJ65
♣ AQJ

East
♠ Q876
♥ 3
♦ K72
♣ 65432

South
♠ A54
♥ QJ764
♦ A43
♣ K7

South	West	North	East
1♥	Dbl	4♥	All Pass

Opening lead: ♠J

Declarer wins in dummy, crosses to the ♠A and runs the ♥Q; a spade is ruffed in the dummy, and the ♥A brings the ♣2 from partner. Your moment is coming. Declarer runs the ♦10 to your jack, partner playing the deuce. At this point there is only one card you can play to defeat this contract, the ♦Q. (A small diamond won't do, it will force partner's king, and you will be the thrown in with a third diamond to lead a club.) Your unblock allows PARTNER to win the third round of diamonds and push a club through declarer. Does your partner realize what a great player you are? Does anybody? (The West hand was defended by the late, great Meyer Schleiffer).

517* To avoid leading the critical suit, you may have to make an unblock in another suit.

Both sides vul.
Dealer South

North (dummy)
♠ K932
♥ 432
♦ 652
♣ K98

West (you)
♠ 65
♥ QJ9
♦ KJ7
♣ J6432

East
♠ 4
♥ 10765
♦ 109843
♣ Q107

South
♠ AQJ1087
♥ AK8
♦ AQ
♣ A5

South	West	North	East
2♣	Pass	2♦	Pass
2♠	Pass	3♠	Pass
3NT*	Pass	4♣**	Pass
4♦**	Pass	4♠	Pass
5♥**	Pass	5♠	Pass
6♠	All Pass		

* Balanced slam-try, forcing.
** Cue bids

Opening lead: ♥Q

Partner plays the ♥7 at trick one, indicating an equal honor, and declarer wins the ace. Declarer draws two trump, partner discarding a low diamond, strips the clubs and cashes the ♥K. If you fail to unblock the jack, you will be thrown in with a heart and forced to lead a diamond (or give declarer a ruff and a sluff). If you unblock, partner can win the heart exit and lead a diamond through declarer. Declarer was very friendly. Had she played the ♥K sooner, you would have had to show your "unblocking flair" earlier.

518* When partner leads the jack from length and you have KQx, unblocking early leads to a more fluid end position, particularly if this turns out to be the throw-in suit.

North-South vul.
Dealer South

North (dummy)
♠ Q1098
♥ QJ65
♦ Q107
♣ 85

West (you)
♠ KJ43
♥ 102
♦ AKJ2
♣ KQ7

East
♠ 1065
♥ 98
♦ 9
♣ J109432

South
♠ A2
♥ AK743
♦ 8643
♣ A6

South	West	North	East
1♥	Dbl.	2♥	Pass
Pass	Dbl.	3♥	All Pass

Opening lead: ♦A

You continue with the king and a diamond, partner ruffing. When partner exits with the ♣J to the ace, unblock the king retaining flexibility in the suit. Later, after declarer ruffs dummy's last diamond, draws trump and exits a club, you can play low allowing partner to win and lead a spade.

519* When you have been thrown-in AFTER the hand has been stripped, yielding a ruff and a sluff might be better than leading the critical suit. Now the bad news: You have to count to know which is better.

Both sides vul.
Dealer South

North (dummy)
♠ A1054
♥ Q4
♦ 643
♣ Q732

West
♠ Q32
♥ 109872
♦ K8
♣ A65

East (you)
♠ J6
♥ K653
♦ QJ1092
♣ J4

South
♠ K987
♥ AJ
♦ A75
♣ K1098

South	**West**	**North**	**East**
1NT	Pass	2♣	Pass
2♠	Pass	3♠	All Pass

Opening lead: ♥10

Declarer cashes two hearts and plays ace-king and a spade to partner's queen as you smartly discard the ♦Q. Partner exits with the king and a second diamond to declarer's ace. When declarer exits with a third diamond, the ball is in your court. Counting tells you that clubs are 4-4 so a ruff and a sluff won't help declarer, breaking clubs may. Play a heart and let declarer tackle the clubs. (A diamond return gives partner a chance to make a mistake and discard a club.)

520* When you have been thrown-in and you must break the critical suit and it appears that you and partner have the jack and queen between you, attack with an honor holding Jx(x)(x), Qx(x)x). (See tip 512)

East-West vul.
Dealer West

North (dummy)
♠ AK94
♥ A1092
♦ KQJ
♣ 76

West
♠ -
♥ J53
♦ 863
♣ AK109432

East (you)
♠ Q106
♥ Q64
♦ A975
♣ QJ8

South
♠ J87532
♥ K87
♦ 1042
♣ 5

West	**North**	**East**	**South**
3♣	Dbl.	3NT	4♠
All Pass			

Opening lead: ♣K

Declarer ruffs the second club, crosses to a trump and leads the ♦K to your ace. You exit a diamond, partner showing an odd number. Declarer cashes a second high trump, a third diamond, and exits a trump to your queen. You have a complete count. Declarer is known to have three hearts presumably headed by the king. If you lead a low heart, partner's jack will drive out the ace and declarer will run the ♥10 through you. (She'll have no choice). However, if you exit with the ♥Q, declarer must guess who has the jack.

521* When faced with a choice of apparent evils after being thrown in:
(1) giving declarer a ruff and a sluff.
(2) leading the critical suit.
(3) leading from an honor into a known tenace position. COUNT!

Both sides vul.
Dealer South.

North (dummy)
♠ AKQ10
♥ J10653
♦ 32
♣ K4

West (you)
♠ 5
♥ KQ2
♦ Q974
♣ J10932

South	West	North	East
1♦	Pass	1♥	Pass
1♠	Pass	4♠	All Pass

Opening lead: ♣J

Partner wins the first two clubs with the Ace and Queen and shifts to the ♦8, declarer wining the ace. After cashing two high spades, declarer runs the jack of hearts into your hand, partner playing the eight. What now?

As declarer is marked with three hearts, her original distribution must be 4-3-4-2. In addition, declarer appears to have started with ♥A9x and ♦ AKJ10.

All you really want to do is preserve your heart winner for the setting trick. If you lead a club or a heart you will lose your heart trick. A diamond return is best because it gives away nothing.

Declarer's hand: ♠ J982 ♥ A94 ♦ AKJ10 ♣ 65
Partner's hand: ♠ 7643 ♥ 87 ♦ 865 ♣ AQ87

522* Any defender who wants respect must be familiar with the "Crocodile Coup" and not fall victim to it.

Both vul.
Dealer North

North (dummy)
♠ 1084
♥ AJ109
♦ KJ6
♣ A72

West (you)
♠ KJ765
♥ 53
♦ 10987
♣ J9

North	**East**	**South**	**West**
1♣	Pass	1♥	Pass
2♥	Pass	4NT	Pass
5♥	Pass	5NT	Pass
6♦	Pass	6♥	All Pass

Opening lead: ♦10

Dummy takes the first trick with the jack, partner playing the deuce. Declarer crosses to the ♠A, draws two trump, partner following, and then two more rounds of diamonds, partner still following. Declarer continues with the ♣K, the ♣A and a club ruff in the closed hand. Are you counting? Dummy remains with the ♠108 and two trump and you have ♠KJ7 and a diamond. Declarer exits with a low spade. Which spade do you play?

Play the KING! Declarer started with three spades and surely would not be playing this way with ♠AQx. Partner must be down to the blank queen. If you play any spade other than the king, partner will be endplayed upon winning the queen. The play is called the "Crocodile Coup" because you have to open your jaws and snare partner's blank honor.

Declarer's hand: ♠ A93 ♥ KQ872 ♦ AQ4 ♣ K8
Partner's hand: ♠ Q2 ♥ 64 ♦ 532 ♣ Q106543

(15)
CARD COMBINATIONS

It is much easier for the declarer to manage a card combination than a defender. After all, declarer gets to see partner's hand. A defender must use inferences and imagination to visualize partner's hand when attacking a suit.

The card one attacks with later in the hand may be FAR removed from the one that is led on opening lead. The number of tricks needed in the suit dictates which card to lead.

BLOCKING AND UNBLOCKING

523. Partner's honor holding in a suit can often be inferred from declarer's play in the suit.

North (dummy)
10954

West (you)
KQJ6

East
A32

South
87

After the king holds, partner must have the ace, so lead low to unblock the suit. If declarer had the ace, she would have taken the trick to ensure a second stopper.

524. Versus notrump when attacking a suit in which you suspect (or need) partner to have greater length than you, unblock your high honors early.

North (dummy)
86

West (you)
KQJ2

East
A7543

South
109

Play the K,Q, and J if you suspect partner has a four or FIVE card suit

525* Keep unimportant suits unblocked.

North (dummy)
954

West (you)
Q103

East
AKJ872

South
6

Versus suit, you lead low to the king. When partner continues with the ace, unblock the queen to keep the suit fluid. You never know what is going to develop.

526* When a conventional spot card return may cost a trick, don't be a slave to rules: return a non-conventional card.

(a)

North (dummy)
964

West
Q8732

East (you)
K105

South
AJ

Partner, with a likely five card suit, leads low to the king and ace. When next on play, return the five rather than the "conventional" ten. If declarer has AJ doubleton, you cannot afford to return the ten.

(b)

North (dummy)
1054

West
K9732

East (you)
AJ6

South
Q8

When partner leads low, with a likely five card suit, win the ace and return the six. You cannot afford to "waste" the jack if declarer has Qx.

527* When a suit is blocked, attack the entry of the hand that has the greater length in the blocked suit.

East-West vul.
Dealer West

North (dummy)
♠ 72
♥ QJ
♦ AKJ1083
♣ 976

West (you)
♠ AKQ85
♥ 10765
♦ Q2
♣ A2

East
♠ 10943
♥ 2
♦ 76
♣ Q108543

South
♠ J6
♥ AK9843
♦ 954
♣ KJ

West	North	East	South
1♠	2♦	3♠*	4♥
All Pass			

* Preemptive

Opening lead: ♠Q (Q from AKQ)

After you cash two spades, you can see that the trump suit is blocked. If you exit with ace and a club removing declarer's hand entry prematurely, declarer will not be able to exit dummy to draw your remaining trump; you ruff the third diamond and you overruff the third club.

STRATEGY

528. When declarer has a REPEATABLE finesse, it is almost always right to duck the first finesse... calmly.

(a)

North (dummy)
QJ105

West (you)
K83

East
762

South
A94

If you duck the queen and win the jack, the suit is blocked.

529. Do not refuse a finesse if partner is likely to hold an equal honor in the suit. Winning will force declarer to use an extra entry to repeat the finesse.

North (dummy)
J1093

West (you)
K87

East
Q62

South
A54

If the jack is led and ducked, take the trick. Either the suit is blocked (declarer having started with AQx), or declarer will need TWO additional dummy entries both to repeat the finesse and run the suit.

LEADING UNUSUAL CARDS

530* When attacking a suit in which you need four tricks and both LHO and partner have four cards, attack with your LOWER honor holding two UNEQUAL honors and a THREE card holding.

North (dummy)
8654

West (you)
A103

East
KQ72

South
J9

If you are going for FOUR tricks in this suit (notrump), attack with the ten. (Attack with the nine from A9x, K9x, or Q9x). If partner attacks with the king, unblock the ten (or nine). (See tip 398, example two).

531* When LHO and partner each have four cards, leading high from 10xx, Jxx or Qxx frequently saves a trick when RHO has honor doubleton.

North (dummy)
KQ92

West (you)
J54

East
10763

South
A8

Attack with the jack and save a trick.

When attacking a suit in which you and RHO each have four cards and dummy has 10x, Jx, or Qx, attack with the higher of two honors if you need FOUR tricks. Partner, with a hoped for honor third, must cooperate by unblocking a significant middle card.

North (dummy)
Q5

West (you)
KJ82

East
A93

South
10764

At notrump needing FOUR tricks, start with the king and hope partner unblocks with the nine. This allows you to lead low to the ace and remain with the J8 over declarer's 107. (If partner leads the suit the nine must be led initially.

533* When you need partner to hold particular card with particular length, do not hesitate to lead an unusual card to cater to your needs

(a)

North (dummy)
9876

West
A32

East (you)
QJ105

South
K4

Versus notrump, if you need FOUR tricks, attack with the five. You can't afford to lead an honor, you need all of your honors to beat dummy's spot on the fourth round of the suit; lead the five from KJ105 or AJ105 for the same reason.

(b)

North (dummy)
954

West
A6

East
KQ1032

South
J87

Versus. notrump, lead low if you need FIVE tricks. Leading high blocks the suit when partner has Ax.

534* When leading through a king in a CASH OUT situation, the lead of a low card promises either the queen or the ace.

North (dummy)
K1076

West
2

East (you)
AJ54

In a "cash out" position (you must take as many tricks as quickly as possible) play the jack if dummy plays low— partner must have the queen. With 982 or 9832, partner's should lead the nine.

535* When trying to build up a trick in a suit in which LHO is known to be strong, lead low from a doubleton honor. Preserve your honor so partner can return the suit safely when she gets in.

(a)

North (dummy)
AQ105

West (you)
K7

East
J843

South
962

If your side needs one trick and you have no outside entry, attack with the seven. Even if declarer plays the queen, a trick can be developed if partner has two entries. Lead the king and you cannot develop a trick.

(b)

North (dummy)
AK106

West (you)
J3

East
Q752

South
984

Attack with the three if you need one trick and have no quick outside entry; play the same with Qx.

(c)

North (dummy)
765

West
A102

East (you)
J3

South
KQ984

Assume this is the trump suit and your aim is to play two quick rounds. Lead the 3. Play the same with 10x, Qx or Kx.

SURROUNDING PLAYS

536* When RHO has 10x(x) and you have the ten "surrounded"with the AJ9(x) or the KJ9(x), attack with the jack.

(a)

	North (dummy)	
	1075	
West		**East** (you)
K32		AJ96
	South	
	Q84	

Play the same with AJ8x and hope partner has K9x. Note: Surrounding plays are based on declarer's likely length.

(b)

	North (dummy)	
	104	
West		**East** (you)
932		KJ876
	South	
	AQ5	

Attack with the jack and hope partner has 9x, 9xx or A9x.

537* Surrounding plays are "off" when LHO is KNOWN to have a doubleton. Lead low if dummy has three cards; high if dummy has four.

	North (dummy)	
	1054	
West		**East** (you)
A763		KJ82
	South	
	Q9	

Leading the jack in this position not only costs you a trick, but, perhaps, a partner as well; lead low. Give dummy partner's trey and you have to attack with the king to realize four quick tricks.

538. When RHO has 9x(x) and you have the nine "surrounded" with the Q108(x), K108(x) or A108(x) attack with the ten.

(a)

	North (dummy)	
	96	
West		**East** (you)
K752		Q1084
	South	
	AJ3	

Lead the ten and declarer gets one trick; lead low and she can get two by ducking.

(b)

North (dummy)
A96

West
K32

East (you)
Q1085

South
J74

Another variation; attacking with the ten limits declarer to one trick. If you lead low and declarer plays low, she comes to two tricks.

FROZEN SUITS

539. A "frozen suit" has nothing to do with clothing stores in Alaska: it has to do with a suit that cannot be attacked by anybody, dummy included, without losing a trick. If, with your bridge genius, you recognize a frozen suit, don't lead it.

(a)

North (dummy)
K65

West (you)
QJ92

East
A74

South
1083

You lead the queen which holds. At this point, the suit is "frozen"- although you may not know it.

(b)

North (dummy)
J108

West
K932

East
Q76

South
A54

After the jack loses to the king, the suit is frozen.

(c)

North (dummy)
J105

West
A932

East
Q76

South
K84

After the jack loses to the ace (or is ducked), the suit is frozen.

THE PLAY WITH EQUALS

540* In order to distinguish honor sequence leads, continue with the lower of three equals if you want partner to overtake or unblock; if you don't want partner to overtake or unblock, or if you only have two equal honors, continue with the adjacent honor.

(a)

North (dummy)
863

West
KQ5

East (you)
A72

South
J1094

Versus notrump when partner leads the king and continues with the queen, do NOT overtake. If partner had KQJx(x) and had wanted you to overtake, partner would have continued with the jack.

(b)

North (dummy)
3

West
KQJ94

East (you)
1052

South
A876

Versus notrump partner leads the king which holds. If partner continues with the jack, unblock the ten. Had partner not wanted an unblock, partner would have continued with the queen.

(c)

North (dummy)
3

West (you)
QJ1084

East
765

South
AK92

You lead the queen which loses to the king. Later you lead the ten asking partner to unblock the nine. If the ten holds, do not continue the suit as declarer is marked with the A9.

541* When an ace must be removed from the dummy quickly and you have the king, you know what you have to do.

Neither side vul.
Dealer **South**

North (dummy)
♠ 42
♥ KQJ1064
♦ A73
♣ 65

West
♠ J8
♥ 852
♦ J92
♣ J10973

East (you)
♠ 5
♥ 973
♦ K854
♣ AK842

South
♠ AKQ109763
♥ A
♦ Q106
♣ Q

South	**West**	**North**	**East**
2♣	Pass	3♥	Pass
3♠	Pass	4♦	Pass
4NT	Pass	5♦	Pass
6♠	Pass	Pass	Pass

Opening lead: ♣**J**

After winning the opening lead your best shot is to switch to the ♦K hoping declarer has the blank ♥A and partner a diamond honor.

INFERENCES

542* Don't defend as if declarer is looking at your hand (unless you are sitting too close to the table or have the habit of holding your cards in a friendly manner). Assume the declarer is making normal, not clairvoyant, plays.

(a)

North (dummy)
9754

West (you)
K6

East
A

South
QJ10832

If this is the trump suit and South leads the queen, play partner for the ace. Why would declarer lead the queen from the AQ?

(16)
AFTERTHOUGHTS (SUIT CONTRACTS)

543. When that dummy comes down, pause a moment to organize your thoughts before playing to trick one regardless of how automatic your play is. (You should tell your opponents you are doing this). Think about:
(1) The bidding (including partner's).
(2) Declarer's likely strength and distribution.
(3) Reading (and remembering) partner's lead.
(4) How many tricks you need to defeat the contract and where are they likely to come from.
(5) The dummy that declarer bought. Was it good, average or poor? (Are dummy's honors well or poorly placed relative to your honors, etc.?)
(6) A general plan.

544. A discouraging signal is not a command to switch suits, it is a suggestion that you are allowed to overrule.

545** If you and partner lead third best from even and lowest from odd vs suit, consider switching to fourth best when:
(1) You are leading partner's suit and you have NOT supported (10872).
(2) Leading from a suit where the third highest card is the eight or nine (KJ92, Q1083).

In (1) a high-low, given the bidding, will look too much like a doubleton.
In (2) you may cost your side a trick if either opponent has four cards, not to mention partner reading the lead as a doubleton if the bidding has not been revealing.

546. Don't make the beginner's error of thinking a seven or an eight is automatically an encouraging signal. Before you come to any conclusions, CHECK TO SEE HOW MANY (IF ANY) LOWER SPOTS ARE MISSING. You may be in for a shock.

	North (dummy) 532	
West (you) KQ96		**East** 7
	South 4	

Playing standard attitude, plus ace from ace-king, partner's seven is discouraging- it is the lowest missing spot. If your king holds, switch- declarer has both the ace and the jack.

547.

When planning your defense facing a partner who has made a non-vulnerable preempt, consider yourself lucky if partner comes up with one defensive trick.

548* When defending against a squeeze holding guards in two suits, try to protect the suit whose length is to your RIGHT.

549* For a squeeze to operate, entries are needed between declarer and dummy. If there is only one entry (link) between the two hands and it can be removed, no squeeze will be possible.

550. If you can diagnose an Axx(x) suit facing a Kxx(x) suit in the opponents' hands, a switch to this suit usually breaks up an impending squeeze.

551* If a competent declarer throws you in to cash winners you would not have been able to cash on your own, be careful, you are probably squeezing your partner.

552. Don't be so busy signaling count, attitude and suit preference that you forget to play bridge. It is MUCH easier to do well with a player who uses common sense and knows no conventions than one who knows them all but doesn't know when to use them. Amen.

553. When a weak declarer makes a strange looking play, assume an error; when a strong declarer makes the same play, beware, or YOU are about to make an error.

554. When partner doubles a partscore without a strong trump holding, partner is probably planning on doing some ruffing. Keep this in mind when partner makes an opening lead.

555. When partner leads a trump from shortness, she is far more likely to have a doubleton than a singleton. Singleton trump leads are rare, except when the auction demands one (partner passing a one level takeout double).

556. When making a penalty double it is clearly better to have a strongish trump holding (QJx(x), KJx(x) in back of the player with the strong trump suit (almost always the declarer). However, if dummy is known to be poverty stricken, those same trump tricks will hold up in front of the declarer. (She will lack the entries to take any trump finesses).

557. When defending a contract where dummy has all the strength and declarer is dying to get to her hand to take some winning finesses, your job is to prevent declarer from reaching her hand. Forcing dummy to ruff is one technique.

558. Whenever declarer does NOT draw trump immediately, there must be a reason. Guess what you have to do.

559. When faced with several lines of defense, choose the one that gives you a LEGITIMATE chance to defeat the contract as opposed to one that requires declarer to make a mistake. (We're talking "reasonable" declarers here).

560. When faced with several lines of defense, one of which wins in more cases than the other(s), by all means select that one. At least you will be protected in the post-mortem.

561. When you lead from shortness, partner may not be able to distinguish a singleton from a doubleton. Your subsequent signalling should be aimed at clarifying the ambiguity.

You can do this by:

(1) Playing high-low in the trump suit (when holding three or more trump) if you have led from a singleton.

(2) Playing low-high in the trump suit if you have led from a doubleton.

(3) Signaling discouragement when partner leads a high honor in a side suit if you have led from a singleton and want a ruff more than a continuation of partner's suit.

(4) Signaling encouragement when partner leads a high honor in a side suit if you have led from a doubleton and a switch back to your original suit appears disadvantageous.

(17) AFTERTHOUGHTS (NOTRUMP)

562* When driving out the opponent's last stopper in your long suit, give suit preference to show where your outside entry lies.

(a)

North (dummy)
♠ 873

West (you)
♠ KQJ92

East
♠ 65

South
♠ A104

Say you lead the king and then the jack of spades both holding. At this point you can lead the queen, the 9, or the 2 to knock out the ace. The queen shows outside heart strength, the 9, outside diamond strength; and the 2, outside club strength.

(b)

North (dummy)
♠ J86

West (you)
♠ K9732

East
♠ A4

South
♠ Q105

You lead low vs. no trump. Partner wins the ace and returns the four to your king. Once again you have a choice of three cards to play. Each card is suit preference.

563. When declarer has a certain stopper in the suit you have led and you have no outside entry, keep communications open by allowing declarer to win the second round of the suit.

North (dummy)
74

West (you)
A8632

East
K95

South
QJ10

Against a notrump contract you lead the three to the king and ten. When partner returns the nine, allow the queen (or jack) to hold. If partner has an early entry you can run the suit. Play the same if you have led from a four card suit headed by the ace, and the suit is divided 4-3-3-3 around the table.

564. When you are third to play (dummy to your left), and you can take the trick, make sure you can't do better by allowing dummy to take the trick so you can take even more tricks later.

(a)

	North (dummy)	
	K64	
West (you)		**East**
AJ92		853
	South	
	Q107	

If partner attacks with the eight and declarer plays the ten, cover with the jack. You remain with a tenace position over the queen.

(b)

	North (dummy)	
	Q84	
West (you)		**East**
AJ105		?
	South	
	?	

This is a tricky one. If partner leads low, presumably showing the king, win the ace and return the jack. If partner leads high, denying the king, play the ten keeping the AJ over declarer's king.

565. When the defense has no readily establishable suit, try to kill the opponent's long suit by removing the side entry to the suit; like removing a snake's fangs.

North-South vul.
Dealer South

	North (dummy)	
	♠ A2	
	♥ K5	
	♦ Q108743	
	♣ 742	
		East (you)
		♠ KJ74
		♥ AJ3
		♦ KJ9
		♣ 653

South	**West**	**North**	**East**
1NT	Pass	3NT	All Pass

Opening lead: ♣J

Declarer wins the queen and plays the ace and a diamond, partner discarding a small spade. How do you continue?

Kill the diamond suit; switch to the ♠K.

Declarer's hand: ♠ Q109 ♥ Q974 ♦ A62 ♣ AKQ
Partner's hand: ♠ 8653 ♥ 10862 ♦ 5 ♣ J1098

Even though you concede three spades with your switch, (declarer had two coming anyway), you kill three diamond tricks, a fair tradeoff.

566* The hallmark of a great defender is knowing how to lead... partner by the hand. (A recurring theme in this book).

North (dummy)
♠ AQJ
♥ Q10976
♦ K82
♣ 94

East (you)
♠ 10875
♥ AKJ
♦ 1073
♣ A86

South	**West**	**North**	**East**
1♦	Pass	1♥	Pass
1NT	Pass	3NT	All Pass

Opening lead: ♣ 3
Dummy plays low; plan your defense.

To make things absolutely clear, win the ♣A, cash the ♥K, and then return the ♣8. Your play in hearts indicates AKJ, so if partner has a club winner, a heart return is automatic.

Declarer's hand: ♠ K94 ♥ 54 ♦ AQJ64 ♣ QJ10
Partner's hand: ♠ 632 ♥ 832 ♦ 95 ♣ K7532

567. If the dummy has a TWO loser suit {QJ10x(x), KJ10x(x)}, facing a small doubleton and there is one side entry to dummy, duck the FIRST round of the suit.

North (dummy)
♠ K83
♥ 853
♦ K10986
♣ 74

West
♠ J10952
♥ 106
♦ 75
♣ 10832

East (you)
♠ 74
♥ QJ97
♦ AQ32
♣ QJ9

South
♠ AQ6
♥ AK42
♦ J4
♣ AK65

South	**West**	**North**	**East**
2NT	Pass	3NT	All Pass

Opening lead: ♠J

Declarer wins the first spade with the queen and runs the ♦J. If you take this trick (you wouldn't dream of it), declarer has an easy road to ten tricks by establishing three diamond tricks using the ♠K as the reentry. If you duck the first diamond, declarer winds up with one diamond trick instead of three, eight tricks instead of ten.

568* Watch those spot cards! Don't get lazy!

(a)

North (dummy)
97

West (you)
K10865

East
AQ

South
J432

Defending 3NT with a certain outside entry, you lead the six. When partner wins the ace and returns the queen, overtake and drive out the jack to insure FOUR tricks. (Partner is likely to have AQ doubleton; from AQx, the normal play at trick one is the queen.

(b)

North (dummy)
5

West (you)
AJ943

East
K82

South
Q1076

You lead the four to the king and six. When partner returns the EIGHT to the ten and jack declarer must remain with the guarded queen. If partner returns the deuce showing four, (or two!) declarer's queen is due to fall under the ace.

569. Upside down count (low from four, high or middle from three) is superior to standard count when signaling with a FOUR card suit because you can play your lowest card without wasting anything, (K108x, J107x). However, standard count is superior when holding three cards when the middle card is too valuable to use as a count card (J10x, K10x, KJx etc.)

570* To simplify the defense, when your side needs three tricks shift to the ace from Axx or the king from Kxx playing partner for Kxxx(x) or Axxx(x). Partner, with no side entry must cooperate by ducking the second round of the suit. If you lead low and partner plays high, the suit is lost.

East-West vul.
Dealer West

North (dummy)
♠ KJ106
♥ AK
♦ 1094
♣ 10986

West (you)
♠ Q4
♥ J754
♦ A86
♣ AQ32

East
♠ 9832
♥ 932
♦ K532
♣ 74

South
♠ A75
♥ Q1086
♦ QJ7
♣ KJ5

West	**North**	**East**	**South**
1♣	Pass	Pass	1NT (11-14)
Pass	2NT	Pass	3NT
All Pass			

Opening lead: ♥4

Partner plays the discouraging ♥2 at trick one and a "count" ♣7 at trick two as declarer runs the ♣10 to your queen. All indications point to declarer having the ♠A (four tricks), the ♥Q (three tricks) and the ♣KJ (two tricks once the ♣A is removed) for a grand total of nine. DIAMONDS must be attacked.

As you need to find partner with Kxx(x) or Qxxxx, attack with the ACE and then the eight. If partner is alert (read, awake) partner will duck the second diamond hoping you have a third. When you get in with the ♣A, your follow up of a third diamond allows partner to cash two diamonds to defeat the contract.

571. A happier life awaits you if you have never heard of the Foster Echo. If you have, forget you have.

572* The Smith Echo has far more merit. Briefly, it is used at trick two against notrump. After declarer wins the opening lead and attacks another suit, each defender, if practical, signals attitude towards the OPENING LEADER'S suit. There are too many versions to go into here.

573. If the only way to defeat a contract is to assume declarer has made a mistake or will make one, go for it. NOBODY is perfect, NOBODY.

574. If it is clear that the contract is going to be defeated, set your aim upon extracting the greatest penalty possible, particularly vs. doubled contracts.

575. When declarer remains with only one stopper in your long suit and has two aces to knock out, be wary of letting declarer steal a trick in one of those ace suits before she reverts to the other. This tips assumes you have the setting tricks in your long suit.

(18)
AFTERTHOUGHTS (GENERAL)

576* Do not take your eye off the ball by focusing all of your attention on one suit to the exclusion of the entire hand; a trap that is easy to fall into.

East-West vul.
Dealer South

North (dummy)
♠ 72
♥ KJ63
♦ A1075
♣ 943

East
♠ 864
♥ AQ108
♦ K3
♣ Q1087

South	**West**	**North**	**East**
1♠	Pass	1NT	Pass
4♠	All Pass		

Opening lead: ♦2 (Third and lowest)

Declarer plays low from dummy, you win the king and declarer plays the queen. Now what?

Notice your club holding. Do you remember your surrounding plays? If so, you probably switched to the ♣10 hoping declarer had AJx and partner Kxx. Guess what? Declarer does have AJx and partner does have Kxx and you have just let declarer make an unmakeable hand. Why? Because you forgot to look at the whole hand.

Partner has apparently led from a five card suit and declarer has unblocked with Qx preparatory to finessing the ♦10 after drawing trump. Your play is to kill the dummy at once by returning a DIAMOND. With no side dummy reentry, declarer is forced to try to cash the ♦A at trick three. No luck, you ruff and your club winners come later.

Declarer's hand: ♠ AKQ10953 ♥ 2 ♦ Q8 ♣ AJ5
Partner's hand: ♠ J ♥ 9754 ♦ J9642 ♣ K62

If you return the ♣10 at trick two, declarer wins the ace, draws trump and leads a diamond to the ten; seven spades, two diamonds and a club comes to ten.

577. If you like this book, go over the "good stuff" with your favorite partner(s). Sound defensive play requires partnership agreement, cooperation and TOLERANCE.